D1797789

978 0273 43 1114

A
STUDENT'S REVIEW
OF
PITMAN'S SHORTHAND
DICTATION BOOK

Being the Key to
A Student's Review of Pitman's Shorthand

NEW ERA EDITION

REVISED EDITION

LONDON
SIR ISAAC PITMAN & SONS LTD.

SIR ISAAC PITMAN & SONS LTD.
PITMAN HOUSE, PARKER STREET, KINGSWAY, LONDON, W.C.2
THE PITMAN PRESS, BATH
PITMAN HOUSE, BOUVERIE STREET, CARLTON, MELBOURNE
20-25 BECKETT'S BUILDINGS, PRESIDENT STREET, JOHANNESBURG

ASSOCIATED COMPANIES
PITMAN MEDICAL PUBLISHING COMPANY LTD.
46 CHARLOTTE STREET, LONDON, W.I

PITMAN PUBLISHING CORPORATION
20 EAST 46TH STREET, NEW YORK, N.Y. 10017

SIR ISAAC PITMAN & SONS (CANADA) LTD.
(INCORPORATING THE COMMERCIAL TEXT BOOK COMPANY)
PITMAN HOUSE, 381-383 CHURCH STREET, TORONTO

MADE IN GREAT BRITAIN AT THE PITMAN PRESS, BATH
F5—(S.556)

CONTENTS

iii

THE material in this book is counted in tens for dictation purposes. It is not graded, but in each section special emphasis is placed upon a particular principle of Pitman's Shorthand.

Each section has three subdivisions: "A" which uses only words occurring in the Pitman List of 700 most common words; "B" which extends the vocabulary and covers about 2000 words; and "C" which draws upon a much wider vocabulary and is designed to extend the students' knowledge of words. Each subsection contains a list of words for drill purposes.

SECTION ONE: HOOKS eL AND aR

PART ONE: Hooks eL and aR to Straight Strokes

"A." Vocabulary for Outline Drill

able	bread	paper	tell	member
black	perhaps	increase	till	remember-ed
blue	present	October	deliver-ed-y	number-ed
clear	product	quarter	deliverance	equal-ly
place	trust	water	larger	call
agree	dress	direct	largely	care
April	credit	record	gold	school
break	table	course	great	probable-y-ility
brought	employ	supply	people	danger
drink	political	possible	principle-al-ly	production
girl	trouble	strange	dear	productive
grow	better	industry	during	
true	degree	belief-ve-d	truth	
across	labour	balance	child	

Dictation Practice

(1) The child did not take the direct course to the[10] school. Breaking the rule made by her mother, she walked[20] along by the side of the water, which looked so[30] clear and blue on this perfect morning in April. As[40] she walked she grew warmer, and it seemed the most[50] natural and agreeable course possible for the little girl to[60] sit on the bank of the river where she was[70] able to put her feet into the clear cold water.[80] She remembered, of course, that her dress must be kept[90] clean, for had not her mother ironed it so carefully[100] that very morning? Across the water she could see a number[110] of other little girls, all strange to her. They were[120] breaking bread into little pieces, which they let fall into[130] the water. "Perhaps there are some fish across there," she[140] thought. Lost in a little train of thought, she could[150] not tell how long she had been sitting there; but[160] by degrees the blue of the April day gave place[170] to black, and the child remembered the cares of school.[180] "If I go now I shall probably get into trouble[190] with teacher," she thought. "Perhaps it would be better for[200] me to wait till I see the children coming out[210] of school, and then I can go home with them." (220)

(2) Dear Sirs, It is with regret that we have to[10] inform you that, owing to the greatly increased demand for[20] our special kinds of paper, it will not be possible[30] for us to supply you immediately with all the material[40] for which you ask. The amounts and qualities of paper[50] which we can supply are stated at the foot of[60] this letter. We are also faced with labour troubles just[70] now, a number of our employees having left to work[80] for another organization. We have had to cut production considerably,[90] and it appears that our

organization is about to pass[100] through a more difficult time than any on record for[110] a great number of years. The question of delivery is[120] also a matter largely outside our direct control. We will[130] however undertake to supply half in the early part of[140] the October quarter and the balance during November or December.[150] This is the best we can do for the present,[160] and we trust that you will understand the position in[170] which we are placed. Yours truly, (176)

(3) As Members, you will be pleased to be told that[10] the accounts placed before you to-day show a larger balance[20] than was thought probable a few months ago. In October[30] last I expressed the belief that there was a great[40] danger that when we met here in April the balance[50] to our credit would be the lowest on record. You[60] will therefore all agree with me that the figures we[70] now present to you are better than could have been[80] expected, but this is largely owing to the large sums[90] brought in from last year, and it is true to[100] say that we cannot look for equally satisfactory figures during[110] the present year if there is no increase in productive[120] industry generally. Although it appears that there is trouble in[130] all parts of the world at the present time, your[140] Directors will continue by all means in their power to[150] keep the profit position satisfactory. There are, however, certain things[160] over which the Directors have little or no direct control.[170] While, therefore, you may put your trust in the Directors,[180] you should also remember that they will probably meet with[190] unexpected difficulties and setbacks in the course of the coming[200] months. (201)

" B." Vocabulary for Outline Drill

club	approximate	bitter	proper	college
cloud	addressed	capture	tray	carbon
cloth	group	claim	propose	parcel
glad	broad	church	trench	physical
glass	pretty	corner	terms	extreme
apple	Christmas	crack	trip	destroy
applied	problem	crime	prove	explain
blow	including	copper	kettle	disclose
class	battle	court	angry	stream
close	total	cream	chemical	strength
clock	double	critic	parallel	spread
clothes	couple	breath	feeble	extra
clothing	enclosing	crowd	bottle	sacrifice
grey	sample	dark	uncle	separate
grace	blank	crown	utter	struggle
cross	bless	garden	victor	stretch
draw	neighbour	grip	manager	chair
dream	butter	neutral	prose	cheer
drop	daughter	proceed	angle	doctor
dry	purchase	produce	blade	guard
appreciation	bridge	tree	brick	liberty
promise	bright	trick	collect	practice-se-d
abroad	brook	programme	correct	

Dictation Practice

(4) When the old clock in the College square struck three,[10] Victor closed his books and went out into the grey[20] afternoon. Several groups of boys were standing round the entrance[30] gates, and he addressed them brightly but briefly before he[40] crossed the narrow street. He was on good terms with[50] them all but he did not wish to attract notice.[60] He walked with brisk steps, and soon had crossed the[70] bridge over the stream and entered a small shop in[80] Brook Street. The tinkling of a bell announced his entry.[90] Victor drew a deep breath. From every corner and crack[100] of this little shop there came strange smells, smells which[110] gave the old place a secret charm for persons such[120] as Victor. An old man in shabby grey clothes entered[130] the shop through another door. His watery blue gaze met[140] Victor's eager brown eyes. "So, Master Victor, you have come[150] for your parcel?" He pronounced each syllable very deliberately, and[160] this habit gave all his remarks an air of great[170] importance. "Well, your parcel is ready, but promise me, young[180] man, to be very careful what you do with this[190] little bag of tricks. Otherwise, it's a pretty Christmas you[200] will be having, for sure." He cackled. Victor grabbed his[210] parcel, and, promising to be extra careful, he departed. In[220] a dream he made his way back across the bridge,[230] and came face to face with a couple of men.[240] "My uncle and the doctor," he exclaimed within himself. "Now[250] for it." He must guard his secret from his uncle.[260] He needed more liberty in which to study and practise ;[270] he needed a separate room. Thoughts crowded through his mind,[280] and he felt a passing feeling of discouragement and of[290] physical dislike for the eternal presence of his small brother,[300] with his prying eyes and his love for tricks and[310] practical jokes. "What have you got there, young fellow?" asked[320] his uncle cheerfully. It was extremely difficult to refuse to[330] disclose the contents of the parcel. He struggled to think[340] of a reasonable reply but all possible answers sounded feeble[350] even to himself. He knew only one thing—he must[360] guard the secret of the parcel. Across the road strolled[370] a school chum. Victor called out loudly to attract his[380] attention, muttered something to his uncle and the doctor, and[390] ran quickly across to his friend.   (396)

(5) Messrs. John Brooks and Grace, 27 Glass Street, Glasgow.[10] Dear Sirs, We are enclosing, as promised, samples of several[20] lines of our new spring cloth. We are able to[30] offer you particularly low terms for the cloth due to[40] the very large purchases of material which we made recently.[50] The two colours most in demand for gentlemen's suits this[60] spring are blue and grey. As the samples show, the[70] shade of blue favoured this year is slightly brighter than[80] the dark navy which has been popular recently, and I[90]

think that customers generally will appreciate this change. We have[100] taken the liberty of including with the samples one or[110] two pieces of ladies' suiting. We draw your particular notice[120] to No. 14A., a cloth with a grey background[130] crossed with a faint red check. In our view this[140] particular material will prove extremely popular with the ladies this[150] spring. We shall be glad to supply you with suitable[160] lengths of any of these cloths on receipt of your[170] order. We can promise early delivery of material ordered during[180] this month. Assuring you of our best attention at all[190] times, We are, Yours truly, (195)

(6) Mr. Chairman, Gentlemen, We meet to-day under a dark cloud.[10] There is abroad in all parts of the world a[20] feeling that difficult and perhaps dangerous times are ahead. We[30] in this country have tried to walk with grace, to[40] count our blessings, and to love our neighbours; but we[50] have found ourselves drawn into battle. It is simple to[60] turn critic and to talk bitterly of the crime which[70] is being committed in the name of freedom, but to[80] utter such words is to court trouble. I do not[90] wish to-day to make a political speech and my main[100] purpose is to disclose to you the proposed present and[110] future plans of this great undertaking. I can however claim[120] that the present position is without parallel in history, and[130] no sacrifice, no struggle, is too great if the outcome[140] is to destroy the forces of evil which disgrace civilization[150] and to build that brave new world which we all[160] so eagerly await. (163)

" C." Vocabulary for Outline Drill

blanket	progressive	strides	natural	prospectus
bliss	paragraphs	extricate	prominent	prospect
blisters	trips	destroyed	permanent	prospective
Birmingham	prison	extremely	pre-eminent	characteristic
glory	preclude	blocked	proportion-ed	practicable
propaganda	grapple	blockade	description	democracy
profess	duplicate	granted	incorporated	project-ed
proud	conjurer	guaranteed	neglect-ed	stranger
proof	harbour	garden	preliminary	legislature
Preston	parallels	guardian	telegram	legislator
Bristol	splendidly	neutral	telegraphic	

Dictation Practice

(7) A neglected pamphlet lay on my knees. The propaganda it[10] contained incorporated all that is characteristic of the literature put[20] out by prominent and pre-eminent people who seek to become[30] the guardians of our political interests. I discounted the propaganda[40] in proportion to its impressiveness. Then, too, the glory of[50] the afternoon was such that I was proof against all[60] the propaganda that could be printed by prospective Members of[70] Parliament. I sat back in the garden chair with my[80] hands idle, and

grappled with no problem deeper than whether[90] an approaching white cloud would or would not momentarily blot[100] out the brightness of the sun. Then a bubble drifted[110] past, a glorious coloured soap bubble; then another, larger than[120] the first, carried lightly by the breeze. A third passed,[130] and I could no longer restrain myself. I peeped discreetly[140] over the hedge which separated our garden from the next[150] one. There in a corner behind the bicycle shed sat[160] little Gladys, clasping an old clay pipe to her mouth[170] and nursing a large bowl of soapy water. Gladys was[180] blowing bubbles. For a brief time I was drowned in[190] a rush of happy childhood memories. What hours of delight[200] we had with our little clay pipes and our bowls[210] of soapy water, blowing bubbles into the golden air. What[220] crushing misery it was when we dropped and broke those[230] precious clay pipes! (233)

(8) Peter has done splendid work in Euclid, and I think[10] that a most appropriate and attractive prize for him would[20] be a copy of *Scientific Riddles*, by Professor Sir J.[30] A. Thomson. In his Preface Professor Thomson writes that nature[40] bristles with problems— among the grass and the petals of[50] flowers, in the sea, the sky, everywhere. But the solving[60] of one riddle often discloses another, and the quest continues.[70] Professor Thomson's aim in this book is to select a[80] few fair samples of these scientific riddles and to discuss[90] them so that they suggest others, and so increase the[100] interest of life. There are four sections to the book,[110] and in Part Three a few illustrations of the problems[120] or riddles discussed are: Is telepathy a fact? What lies[130] behind clairvoyance? How explain crystal-gazing? Why do we dream?[140] In Part Four one of the problems tackled is: Is[150] there cruelty in nature? (154)

(9) (*a*) In the preliminary General Knowledge Test we had to make[10] use of parallel rulers, and answer miscellaneous questions regarding the[20] Indian Legislature and the principal factors entitling a people to[30] the description of a democracy. In the geography paper we[40] had to mark on a blank map the towns of[50] Cardiff, Glasgow, Crewe, Middlesbrough, Brighton, Carlisle and Grimsby, and the[60] Rivers Clyde, Trent and Ribble. (65)

(*b*) palpitating pancreas corollary corruptible probationary pro-pitiate gregarious classification palatable plausible irresistible complacent sceptical scrupulously supplementary precursor incalculable

PART TWO: Hooks eL and aR to Curves

" A." Vocabulary for Outline Drill

ever	differ	further	official	their, there
front	cover	weather	shilling	sure
offer	fly	final	fisher	nor
free	brother	measure	wisher	near
other	develop	north	banker	pleasure
through	before	engineer	thinker	mere, Mr.
comfort	Friday	frequent	over	more, remark-ed
friend	discover	Thursday	however	remarkable
either	beautiful	summer	from	
three	river	personal	very	

Dictation Practice

(10) Mr. A. C. Fisher, Fisher Brothers, 134[10] North Street, Wells. Dear Mr. Fisher, Since your call here[20] on Thursday last we have been able to give further[30] consideration to the question of the housing development plans. I[40] have pleasure in informing you that our Mr. Rivers made[50] a personal call upon the Chief Engineer and, to our[60] very great surprise, received from him an offer to call[70] an official meeting very shortly. This offer is the more[80] remarkable inasmuch as the Chief Engineer has frequently seemed to[90] differ from us in his views, and purposely to fly[100] in the face of possible developments put forward by us.[110]

Further, as a final attempt to make sure that something[120] would be done shortly to improve the position, Mr. Rivers[130] called upon three officials, who are personal friends of his,[140] to discover the official view of the measures we have[150] in mind. His report is not yet ready but I[160] think you can take comfort from the knowledge that things[170] will be set moving before the end of the summer.[180] Mr. Rivers expects to have his report ready in its[190] final form by Friday next, and you may be sure[200] that I will send a copy to you as soon[210] as I can. Yours very truly, J. D. Summers. (219)

" B." Vocabulary for Outline Drill

efforts	gather	dinner	civil	impress
fruits	silver	sharper	simmer	imports
flame	hammer	forget	designer	pressure
frame	farmer	former	personalities	initial
afraid	approval	freight	finger	universe
throw	travel	fresh	drinker	university
average	channel	fright	hamper	chairs
Jeffery	honour	moral	hampered	cheers
freeze	humour	original	pamper	chaired
favour	roughly	leather	pampered	cheered
flat	French	thread	linger	
flow	manner	throat	lingered	
flag	furnish	normal	umbrella	
flower	minor	verses	impulse	

Dictation Practice

(11) Mr. Sharp said: Gentlemen, I am afraid that our Director,[10] Mr. French, is unable to take his place in the[20] chair this afternoon

owing to pressure of work, and it[30] has fallen to me to have the honour of filling[40] that position. While the figures given in the accounts are[50] not up to our normal or average standard, they are,[60] I think, sure to receive your approval. You will not[70] forget that formerly we were able to import freely plentiful[80] supplies of material for manufacture into feeding stuffs, which were[90] then bought by farmers throughout the country. This channel of[100] activity is now closely controlled. Further, we have to furnish[110] the authorities with so many details of minor transactions that[120] we are greatly hampered in the carrying out of our[130] normal business. This year represents the Silver Jubilee of the[140] formation of your company, which originally carried the name of[150] the University Fruit and Flower Supply Company. We have travelled[160] far since those days, however, and while we may suffer[170] from slight hampering restrictions, we are cheered by the knowledge[180] that we are bound sooner or later to recover our[190] former position in relation to the farmers. In view of[200] present difficulties we have thrown over our plan to honour[210] the occasion by holding a Jubilee Dinner and Staff Gathering[220] in the Grosvenor. I will not linger on this point,[230] however, but will now furnish you with what is, roughly[240] speaking, a summary of the report and the accounts for[250] the year.   (252)

(12) The average person loves flowers, and it seems to be[10] a natural impulse of the normal child to pick any[20] flowers which come within reach of his exploring fingers. Is[30] there a more delightful sight than to see a city[40] child clinging lovingly to an armful of wild flowers gathered[50] during a day of freedom in the woods and meadows?[60] This widespread love of flowers makes gardening a much-favoured[70] hobby. If you are planning to begin work as a[80] gardener, be sure to find out first which flowers, fruits[90] or vegetables your particular soil favours; do not be afraid[100] to make a generous use of spade and fork; and[110] always use fresh seed or you will hamper your own[120] efforts. Gardening is a hobby which offers great scope for[130] your imaginative faculties; there is almost no limit to the[140] original display which you can make. You can become the[150] designer of a lay-out of lawn and flower-beds which[160] will win the approval of your most critical friends. Do[170] not be afraid to seek the advice of leading seedsmen[180] and market gardeners. They are all ready to offer you[190] good advice. If the initial work in the garden is[200] heavy, the return is great; and as you sit in[210] your deckchair during a long summer evening, listening to the[220] throaty notes of the blackbird and the thrush, or watching[230] the graceful butterfly as it flutters lightly by or lingers[240] for a moment upon a petal of some flower, you[250] will find your heart glow with pride in your own[260] creation.   (261)

" G." Vocabulary for Outline Drill

affright	floor	humorous	hanger	proffer
fright	flannel	rumour	singer	prefer
averse	rival	suffering	imply	differ
verse	spiteful	civilization	embezzle	defer
ether	eternal	deceiver	embraces	adverse
freights	naval	dishonour	embarrasses	diverse
thrift	generating	camper	fresher	commercial-ly
thrifty	miners	jumper	freshly	mortgage-d
thermometer	morally	tamper	former	bankruptcy
Bradford	abnormal	tampered	firmer	enlightenment
Liverpool	philosophy	hanker	favoured	universal
Wolverhampton	cardinal	hankered	favourite	valuation

Dictation Practice

(13) I prefer to differ from you in this matter, and[10] if it embarrasses you, as you imply in your letter[20] of the third, I suggest that you defer coming to[30] a decision for a few days. It is morally impossible[40] for me to tamper with the figures given in the[50] valuation. I appreciate that the situation is abnormal, however, and[60] if you are averse from forcing the bankruptcy your best[70] procedure would be to visit your headquarters in Wolverhampton and[80] see whether there are any favourable factors which have not[90] been fully considered. I am mindful of the dishonour which[100] would result from the bankruptcy, and I trust therefore that[110] you will accept the advice which I now proffer you.   (120)

(14) According to one of the fables of Aesop, two men[10] who were travelling together through a thickly wooded jungle promised to[20] stand by each other should any danger threaten them. They[30] had not traversed very much farther before a great bear[40] shambled into sight and immediately rushed at them, growling. Upon[50] this, one of the travellers who was a good climber[60] clambered up into a tree. The other man could not[70] climb, and he fell flat upon his face and lay[80] quite still, holding his breath. The manoeuvre succeeded, for the[90] bear came up and snuffled round him, but supposing him[100] to be dead he departed. When the danger no longer[110] threatened, the man who had clambered up the tree came[120] down and asked his friend what the bear had remarked[130] to him when he was snuffling around so close to[140] his ears. "Why," answered the other, "he advised me to[150] take care in future to put no trust in deceivers[160] like you." And Aesop adds the moral that a true[170] friend will always stand by when danger threatens.   (178)

(15) (a) The initial equipment required for Semaphore signalling is merely two[10] flags. The flags, measuring roughly two feet square, should be[20] differential in colour from the background—the flags being either[30] of a fresh light hue if used in front of[40] a dark background, or of a dark hue if used[50] before a light background. It

is beneficial if the first[60] finger is held strongly against the handle of the flag.[70] When not in use the flags should be dropped vertically[80] downwards in front of the signaller. When displayed they must[90] take one of seven positions, each position differing from its[100] neighbour by half a right-angle. It is essential that[110] these positions are strictly adhered to as small superficial differences[120] may be very important. As the Morse Code can be[130] used under conditions when Semaphore signalling would not be practicable[140] it has more potential value. A very short study of[150] Morse enables a learner to send signals. (157)

(b) manoeuvre fiduciary residential mercenary nurtured thermal Philadelphia fraudulent virulence frivolously virtuous conflagration frustrating malingerer metaphor refraction

SECTION TWO: HOOKS eN AND eF/Vee

PART ONE: Hooks eN and eF/Vee to Straight Strokes

" A." Vocabulary for Outline Drill

clean	one	run	understand	above
plan	open	country	round	chief
plant	between	account	spend	halved
planters	burn	behind	stands	served
plain	down	depend	winter	wonderful-ly
children	learn	ground	once	been
train	modern	kind	distance	general-ly
hundred	question	paint	experience	cannot
begin	town	pointer	experiences	advantage
engine	turn	pound	drive	difficult
June	return	want	perfect	

Dictation Practice

(16) While I do not think that it will serve any[10] useful purpose from your point of view, I am willing[20] to do what you want and to put down in[30] plain language an account of how I spent the morning[40] in question. I took the first down train from town,[50] reaching our station at 9.42. My car was[60] still standing in the yard where it had been left[70] the night before after I drove myself to the station.[80] I set off from the station immediately and had a[90] perfect run for the short distance to my country house.[100] I went round the grounds to look at the growing[110] plants, and while walking round I happened to hear the[120] note of airplane engines overhead. This is no unusual experience[130] in our part of the country, however, and I carried[140] on without turning my head to look up. When I[150] returned to the car I saw that the paint was[160] not clean, so I began to clean it. I frequently[170] clean it myself as it provides me with a profitable[180] way of spending my time. About half an hour later[190] two children ran up behind me. They were so worked[200] up that it was difficult to understand what they had[210] to say but from the account they gave me I[220] learned that an airplane was burning in the field next[230] to my grounds.　　　　　(233)

" B." Vocabulary for Outline Drill

sudden	wind	button	Indian	private
queen	apparent	tin	instant	defeat
foreign	extending	tendency	instance	defend
bond	joining	president	maintain	defence
gain	band	submarine	correspond	grave
cotton	tender	print	correspondence	devote
skin	guns	religion	achieve	prevent
bone	chance	substance	tough	reserve
brown	dance	brain	brave	curve
corn	expense	captain	gift	native
pain	explains	discount	cough	pin
pen	obtains	economy	activity	pony
green	chain	grain	definite	journey
rain	chin	imagine	divide	wavy
count	curtains	incident	advance	
agent	drains	incline	gloves	

Dictation Practice

(17) The legends of the people of past centuries were often[10] centred round natural laws which they could not properly explain.[20] These legends seldom lack interest, and here is one of[30] them. There is an old Indian Legend which explains the[40] universe by maintaining that the sun, the moon, the planets[50] and the stars combine to make up a great family.[60] The sun is the chief or king of the heavens;[70] the moon is his wife and queen, and the stars[80] and planets are their children, the princes. Tender as are[90] the bonds which join the king and the princes, the[100] great chief is apparently obliged to eat any of the[110] little princes he can catch so that he may have[120] enough substance on which to feed. The instant the great[130] chief rises in the morning, therefore, the stars and the[140] planets dance out of his sight and stay hidden till[150] he is tired and inclines once more to his bed[160] in the western part of the heavens. Once a month[170] the moon, his wife and queen, grieves because he has[180] eaten some of the princes who chanced to come in[190] his path, and she draws a black curtain across her[200] face as a proof of her pain and grief. Her[210] grief gradually quietens, however, and her face brightens each day[220] until she is once again radiant. The little princes love[230] the queen, and dance as she joins them again. But[240] after a time there are more disappearances among the princes,[250] and again the queen has to wear mourning to show[260] that she grieves. (263)

(18) Having explained why the expenses of maintaining the estates were[10] heavier than formerly, the President went on: "Our agent, Captain[20] Jones, has just returned from a journey to our cotton[30] plantations, where he was able to devote his undivided attention[40] to our interests and to obtain more definite information regarding[50] the painful incidents and disturbances which occurred last year among[60] the native workers. Captain Jones set off on this journey[70] with a full knowledge of the tough time ahead of[80] him; but he has brains and energy, and he achieved[90] far more than we could have expected during his short[100] stay. He observes that he found the position more grave[110] than we had imagined it to be, but as a[120] definite result of his activities we are confident that we[130] can take measures which will prevent further disturbances this year.[140] I need not explain points in more detail, as a[150] brief summary of our agent's report is contained in the[160] general report which is in your hands to-day. As for[170] the cotton itself, when the Captain left there had been[180] a period of wind and rain which was unusual for[190] the time of year, but the tender cotton shoots were[200] apparently strong enough to withstand the sudden storms, and Captain[210] Jones states confidently that we can count on plentiful crops[220] this season. We propose to draw lightly upon our reserves[230] this

year to meet the expense of some important draining[240] work which must be undertaken without delay. (247)

" C." Vocabulary for Outline Drill

abstain	tendencies	splendour	crofters	expensive
marine	crowned	cantering	drifters	mechanical-ly
spurn	mourned	remittances	waterproof	behalf
privately	ornaments	substances	providence	significance
maintenance	brand	hens	improvident	circumstance
economize	countenance	confidences	devoid	circumstances
accident	standards	pigeons	attorney	defective
Britain	accountancy	prunes	café	imperfect-ion-ly
bending	constant	constructive	abundant	legislative
currency	rendered	conserve	abandoned	negligence
respond	engender	roof	pervade	
responding	ponder	draft	provide	
acquaint	pretender	crave	rain	
acquaintances	encounter	cursive	ruin	

Dictation Practice

(19) A condensed review of our correspondent's report is printed in[10] the current number of *In Britain To-day*. A note of[20] cheerfulness pervades the report, which is certainly not devoid of[30] interest and is likely to cause many readers to ponder[40] over its contents in private. Britain's new aeroplanes apparently show[50] a great improvement upon the kinds now in use in[60] the squadrons. The special significance of this lies in the[70] fact that the types already in existence have already been[80] proved to have speeds greater than those of planes not[90] yet in full production in certain other countries. The inference[100] to be drawn is that the British aeroplane is definitely[110] an advance upon its foreign competitors. This is a point[120] which should be constantly borne in mind when rumours fly[130] round about the high standards of foreign military aircraft. We[140] have abundant proof that our planes come as near to[150] mechanical perfection as can be reasonably expected, and in this[160] country to-day an imperfect or defective machine is practically unknown.[170] We welcome correspondence from our readers on points of general[180] interest but in all the circumstances we think our correspondents[190] would do well to abstain from adverse criticism. Another paragraph[200] which is contained in the current issue of *In Britain[210] To-day* is one relating to the new financial control and[220] its effect upon the trade of certain foreign countries. It[230] is pointed out that shortly after war began certain non-belligerent[240] countries encountered numerous difficulties and so entered into discussions with[250] the belligerent countries with the view to taking steps to[260] ensure that their industries and the people generally should be[270] provided with essential supplies. The export of certain substances was[280] forbidden. But this was not the full extent of the[290] difficulties. Numbers of important oversea products were being retained at[300] various control bases pending further

discussions. Then an agreement was[310] drawn up which provided that trade with the neutral countries[320] should remain unrestricted but export is forbidden by the countries[330] concerned except under guarantee that no contraband products will reach[340] belligerent countries by indirect routes. A rapid turn of circumstances,[350] however, may render the agreement valueless at any time.   (359)

(20) (a) I had almost abandoned hope of retrieving my lost rain-proof.[10] I could not pretend that it was valuable but it[20] had been a constant companion during these wandering days, and[30] in this rainy weather I might easily ruin my expensive[40] new clothes if I were without a waterproof to shield[50] me from the elements. Suddenly I remembered the restaurant where[60] I had taken coffee. I entered the crowded café, and[70] learned at one glance that my torn rainproof was dangling[80] over the chair I had recently vacated. As I bent[90] over to retrieve it I encountered a countenance which frequent[100] meetings during adolescence had rendered well-known to me. I[110] grinned but the once jovial countenance maintained its grave and[120] arrogant expression.   (122)

(b) intolerant allegiance inheritance disruptive encumbrance indigent receptivity improvident sequence incipient ingredient debentures quarantine provocative remunerative suburban hieroglyph adjournment

PART TWO: Hook eN to Curves
" A." Vocabulary for Outline Drill

man	afternoons	million	friends	meant
men	mean	situation	event	payments
often	meaning	woman	front	southern
than	iron	women	land	northern
then	ironed	amount	landing	within
even	line	mind	finder	opinion
evening	lined	demand	finder	
mine	machine	demands	moment	
afternoon	machines	friend	momentary	

Dictation Practice

(21) Special events demand special measures. Now that we can no[10] longer get all the men employees required to keep our[20] machines operating fully, we are finding that it is more[30] than ever necessary to employ women workers to mind our[40] machines. This situation has not come about in a moment,[50] nor is it something new to us, as during the[60] last war we found ourselves in much the same situation.[70] In my opinion, however, the future will see an even[80] greater employment of women than was the case before. Indeed,[90] a statement was recently made that in all probability an[100] additional two million women would be needed for industry before[110]

the end of the year. In this connection there is[120] one question to which we shall have to find an[130] answer, although I am not going to make any statement[140] on it this afternoon, and that is the growing demands[150] made by women that their rate of payment should be[160] equal to that of the men. There are many sides[170] to this question, but in my opinion if the demand[180] is strong enough the women will get what they want.[190] I understand that an agreement on this matter has already[200] been reached in the case of certain women workers, and[210] it is to be expected that other agreements on the[220] same lines will follow within the next few weeks.   (229)

" B." Vocabulary for Outline Drill

shine	lawn	remain	summon	oven
shining	moon	remained	union	ovens
amend	none	England	amusement	fence
around	ocean	examine	remainder	fencing
arrange	fines	fun	settlement	France
oranges	arrangement	fancy	thunder	Westminster
thin	enjoyment	main	founder	leaf
finish	determine	noon	linen	laughs
finished	department	mount	ornament	muffs
fund	silent	mountain	punishment	knives
lean	silently	offence	servant	

Dictation Practice

(22) The young servant remained silent, leaning against the fence which[10] separated the settlement from the smooth lawns. That morning she[20] had, in fun, worn fine linen, had pleased her youthful[30] fancy by covering herself with bright ornament. She had done[40] more than that, too, for she had ventured into her[50] mistress's room and there had examined her unusual appearance in[60] the long mirror in the corner of the room. She[70] had laughed to see herself in so much finery. Offence[80] she had given to none; yet here she was, waiting[90] for the summons which would bring her to some unknown[100] punishment. It was noon, and the sun shone on the[110] fence till it was hot as an oven to the[120] touch, but the thin body of the servant girl shook[130] slightly as she leaned against the fence, dull to the[140] beauty of the orange trees and the wonder of the[150] misty clouds which rested gently on the distant blue mountains.[160] The moments passed slowly, and the summons had not yet[170] come. Her dusky face grew sullen, and her frown deepened.   (180)

" C." Vocabulary for Outline Drill

unions	nouns	equipment	errand	infants
lining	concerning	endowment	renowned	elephant
haven	furniture	Ireland	refunding	invent
bullion	mountainous	island	relents	amendment
infant	tormenting	lens	laments	asunder
leaning	deportment	assent	cementing	Sutherland

reminders	hinterland	offensive	impassioned	abandonment
shunter	Highlanders	Axminster	impatient	appointment
imponderable	vehement	evincing	determined	contentment
calendar	London	annoyance	detriment	attainment
inventors	finance	Scotland	human	financial-ly
islanders	immense	England	humane	assignment

Dictation Practice

(23) Dear Mr. Line, I should like your opinion upon a[10] matter which is of urgent concern to myself and my[20] colleagues. We have in our employment a Mr. Ernest Ireland,[30] who took up an appointment as one of our agents[40] two years ago. His first assignment was to the Sutherland[50] area, and his determined efforts there on our behalf gave[60] him immense financial success. We were impressed with his achievements[70] and yielded to his vehement requests to be given an[80] assignment to our most important area in Scotland in succession[90] to Mr. Munns, whose work had been less brilliant. Since[100] being given the new appointment Mr. Ireland has evinced a[110] most distressing tendency to neglect our interests, and has caused[120] us offence and annoyance by all means in his power.[130] Further, I now believe that he is leaning towards a[140] policy of working deliberately to our detriment. He has ignored[150] our many reminders concerning his duty to us as employers,[160] and we seem unable to do anything to hinder his[170] undesirable activities. We cannot ignore the gravity of the situation,[180] however, and we are impatient to take definite action; but[190] between us and the attainment of our desire to cancel[200] his appointment is the obstacle that he has a very[210] strong contract. It is almost certain that he would go[220] to law rather than assent to the abandonment of the[230] coveted position. At the moment we have not enough authentic[240] facts to make a good impression in a court of[250] law. I can assure you that we are not making[260] a mountain out of a molehill, and I think that[270] a preliminary talk with you would convince you of the[280] need for action and would be immensely useful to us.[290] Yours truly, (292)

(24) (a) Towards the end of the 17th century Captain Cook waved[10] goodbye to England and set off in the good ship[20] *Endeavour.* After numerous experiences he rounded Cape Horn and discovered[30] a group of lovely islands in the great Pacific Ocean.[40] These islands now belong to France and are known as[50] the Society Islands. Bathed in the brilliant sunshine and set[60] in the brilliant blue ocean, these islands looked like fairyland[70] to the men who beheld them. On the low islands[80] grew palm-trees, tall ferns, and brilliantly coloured flowers and shrubs.[90] On the higher islands were sugar canes and fruits. But[100] Captain Cook and his men could not linger, and in[110] time they found their way to the land

called New[120] Zealand, a title given to it years before by a[130] Dutch sailor Tasman. For New Zealanders Christmas Day is a[140] summer festival, held when the flowers are blooming in abundance[150] and the sunshine is radiantly vivid, for the seasons in[160] these southern lands are exactly opposite to ours in the[170] northern hemisphere. Gold, coal, and iron are found in New[180] Zealand.   (181)

(*b*) balloon salient insolvent omniscience predicament cylinder irrelevant sanctioned succulence maligns impediment tannin imminence irreverent calendar discerns interned

SECTION THREE: SHUN HOOK

" A." Vocabulary for Outline Drill

nation	completion	education	reaction	represent-ed
attention	perfection	educational	inaction	representation
division	distribution	operation	information	public-sh-ed
divisional	action	position	generalization	publication
observation	actions	taxation	object	
observations	actionable	taxations	objection	
relation	connection	station	organize-d	
relations	connections	situation	organization	

Dictation Practice

(25) Attention has been called this afternoon by one or two[10] members to the observations made by the Divisional Chief in[20] this connection. I am not at the moment in a[30] position to go forward with the publication of his full[40] report, but after receiving certain information in relation to the[50] organization of our business I formed the opinion that immediate[60] action would be necessary to meet the special situation. Although[70] there were representations from one or two quarters that there[80] might be objections from the employees and that the general[90] reaction would be bad, it was considered that these were[100] mere generalizations, not to be taken too seriously. Our Divisional[110] Chief has not yet brought his work in this connection[120] to a completion, but I can say that it appears[130] from careful observation that the operation of the new taxation[140] is having a bad effect upon distribution of orders after[150] completion. To those in control of this organization, this is[160] a most serious thing, because for years this company has[170] given its first thought to the perfection of its system[180] of distribution, and anything touching this question demands immediate consideration[190] and attention. We have worked hard, and we believe that[200] we have the situation well in hand. Although the rate[210] of taxation is beyond our control it is our opinion[220] that we can influence the method of operation to some[230] degree and so improve the general position. These few observations[240] will show that your Directors are well in control of[250] the special situation. (253)

" B." Vocabulary for Outline Drill

mention	association	occasion	rations	proposition
mentioned	examinations	occasional	applications	physicians
fiction	motion	hesitation	attractions	musician
fashionable	vacation	discussions	electrician	musicians
provisions	affection	section	co-operation	corporation
provisional	affectionate	sectional	decision	destruction
expansion	affectionately	occupation	indecision	
notion	invention	reduction	possession	
examination	selections	repetition	possessions	

Dictation Practice

(26) Dear Cousin Freda, For me this is a most important[10] occasion, and I feel like sitting on cushions and wearing[20] silken robes. As I mentioned in my last communication to[30] you, the final examinations have been held this week, and[40] they came to a conclusion to-day, for which I am[50] very thankful—although I think I have done reasonably well.[60] Of course, the chief topic of conversation at home now[70] is, "What occupation shall I follow?" Actually I have no[80] notion of what I would really like to do, and[90] I cannot come to a decision in spite of the[100] co-operation of my teachers and parents, and in spite of[110] many discussions of a more or less affectionate character. It[120] seems fashionable nowadays to become a writer of fiction. Well,[130] I am not in that particular fashion because I do[140] not like writing and I have no powers of invention.[150] What I would rather like is to be a musician,[160] but that is ruled out because my family will hardly[170] allow me to mention the word *music*. Yesterday I grew[180] tired of these endless discussions and provisionally agreed to think[190] about training to be a physician. Of all the propositions[200] put before me that has the most attraction, but it[210] would be with much hesitation that I took up a[220] career of that kind. It seems to me that the[230] profession of a physician is one to which one should[240] have a natural inclination, not something to be taken up[250] as a matter of casual selection. In addition, I am[260] not at all sure that lady physicians are really popular[270] with the public. However, no final decision is to[280] be forced upon me until I have had a vacation.[290] Now it is about this vacation, not my profession, that[300] I am really writing to you. May I come and[310] stay with you for a little while? I should love[320] to have some real conversation with you again, and particularly[330] to hear your impressions of your last visit to the[340] Continent and your mad rush back in August. I would[350] try not to bother you too much, and I am[360] sure that you would find me very easy to cater[370] for, as I seldom take sugar in my tea, I[380] have no notion whether I am eating butter or margarine,[390] and I never take bacon for breakfast, preferring toast and[400] marmalade, with an occasional egg. I look forward eagerly to[410] your reply. Yours affectionately, Winifred.   (415)

(27) Madam, We regret that you have had occasion to complain[10] of lack of attention to your request. Our premises have[20] been undergoing extensive expansion during the last few months, and[30] the occupation of several new sections was completed only yesterday.[40] While this does not excuse our omission, we trust that[50] it will explain it satisfactorily.

We now have pleasure in[60] enclosing a selection of cushion materials for your consideration and[70] examination. Two of the shades you mention, old gold and[80] crimson, seem to be out of the fashion just now,[90] and we have had no occasion to supply these colours[100] for some time. All the other shades mentioned by you[110] are, however, sent with this letter. We trust that we[120] shall hear further from you in the near future. We[130] are, Yours faithfully,

(133)

"C." Vocabulary for Outline Drill

depreciation	invasion	portion	renovation	investigation
extension	stipulation	duration	evacuation	retrospection
solution	collusion	saturation	punctuation	signification
emotion	admission	discretion	fluctuation	inscription
profusion	commission	precautions	intuition	identification
intimation	desolation	precautionary	composition	introduction
vision	fashions	exclusion	procession	jurisdiction
visionary	location	erections	disposition	amalgamation
missionary	allegations	specification	sensations	justification
tension	Legation	exasperation	cessation	satisfaction
revision	corporations	depression	emigration	
aviation	contraction	agitation	immigration	
privation	election	penetration	passionate	
manipulation	reactionary	plantations	patient	

Dictation Practice

(28) The contention that the time devoted at the special session[10] to a consideration of the location of industry was excessive[20] is a contention which has no foundation in reality. It[30] is an allegation made in a mood of exasperation and[40] without a realization of the facts. An admission was made[50] by the Minister that events have outstripped the publication of[60] the report of the Royal Commission on the Location of[70] Industry, but he had vision enough to agree that the[80] problem is a vital one, and he displayed a complete[90] recognition of the truth that there cannot be an indefinite[100] suspension of the solution. An intimation was given to the[110] House that there would be a consideration of the whole[120] question of post-war reconstruction. Among the opposition, however, there were[130] some who were not prepared to accept the assumption that[140] the Report of the Royal Commission is out of date[150] simply because industry which before the War was uncontrolled as[160] to location is now to a large extent under control[170] both in the matter of location and the allocation of[180] material. Now, they say, is the time to begin an[190] investigation of the probable post-war situation of industry and the[200] redistribution of various industries throughout the country. There was an[210] expression of a similar conviction in the discussion on man-power[220] and the prosecution of the export drive. Here again the[230] contention was that there should be consideration now of the[240] problems which will arise during the transition period ahead of[250] us. Attention was called to the depletion of the building[260] industry's resources during the last war with the result that[270] at the conclusion of hostilities there was widespread disillusionment and[280] desolation. There is, however, a recognition

of the fact that[290] for the present at least it is necessary to move[300] with discretion and precaution, and that the introduction of new[310] measures can be proceeded with only with great caution.   (319)

(29) (*a*) There can be no discussion of the course of evolution[10] without the invasion of strong personal superstitions and passionate emotions.[20] Where there is this intrusion of superstitions and emotions it[30] is difficult to arrive at a solution. Indeed, to ask[40] the question: "Is evolution necessarily upwards?" is a deliberate invitation[50] to heated argument. Out of the profusion of opinions, let us[60] make a selection of only one, and venture to repeat[70] the opinion given expression to by a prominent scientist. Organic[80] evolution, he writes, is not necessarily a progression, but on[90] the whole evolution has been towards greater differentiation and integration.[100] In the course of the ages there have been extinctions,[110] some of which remain very puzzling, degenerations and retrogressions which[120] should act as a warning to man. But taken all[130] round there has been an increase in the freedom of[140] life and a trend towards the emancipation of mind.   (149)

(*b*) condescension animadversion intercession stupefaction vaccination syncopation consummation recession vacillation deterioration cohesion superannuation exemption annihilation tactician incision coercion

SECTION FOUR: eSS AND Zee
(Circle and Strokes)

PART ONE: Circle eSS and Zee

"A." Vocabulary for Outline Drill

sense	history	support	winters	subject
business	successes	sales	spends	subjection
Sunday	persons	signs	chiefs	several
desires	customers	certain	serves	impossible
results	tests	small	afternoons	itself
thousands	discover	yes	friends	influence
meets	safe	wise	machines	is, his
lessens	masters	stations	millions	as, has
answers	expert	serious	nations	myself
six	force	simple	conditions	himself
beds	house	straight	taxation	those, thyself
senseless	Tuesday	strong	positions	this
officers	horse	supplies	special-ly	exchange-d
sits	news	summer	speak	expect-ed
pictures	such	sooner	surprise	
customs	base	once	because	

Dictation Practice

(30) Sirs, Some days ago we sent to your city office[10] two lists setting out the special requirements of our customer,[20] Miss Wise, asking at the same time that these lists[30] should receive expert and early consideration. Two days afterwards we[40] received a few lines from Mr. Small to inform us[50] that matters of this sort are usually seen to by[60] Mr. Strong of the head office and that he was[70] therefore placing the lists before Mr. Strong for his special[80] consideration. We expected to receive some news from Mr. Strong[90] at once, but to our surprise we have since then[100] received nothing. Miss Wise has this morning informed us that[110] she hopes to call at this office personally on Wednesday,[120] the sixth, for the purpose of receiving our considered opinions[130] on the points in question. If we are not in[140] a position to be of service to her in this[150] respect it will certainly result not only in a serious[160] loss of time for her but also in a serious[170] loss of business for us. Can you therefore possibly give[180] us your suggestions by return? Yours truly,   (187)

(31) The house is some two miles from the station, and[10] is smaller and simpler than I had expected it to[20] be, but the grounds are big and its situation generally[30] is most pleasing. The house stands some hundred feet off[40] the road and has fields on all sides. Sometimes in[50] a case of this sort one finds that the windows[60] of the house seem purposely to turn away from the[70] most pleasing views but such is not the case with[80] this house. It has windows on three sides, and because[90] of the nature of the countryside it seemed to me[100] as I went from room to room that the view[110] from each of these windows was better than the view[120] from the others. I

sat in the room for some[130] minutes, waiting for Miss Price, and as I sat there[140] I watched the golden and red leaves falling, as it[150] seemed, in their thousands. It is strange, I thought, that[160] when a person dies the relations or friends put on[170] a black dress to express their regrets, but when the[180] leaves are dying together in their thousands they put on[190] their beautiful dress of many colours. (196)

(32) Dear Sir, I have received your reports of the third[10] and the sixth of September respectively, giving the details of[20] the special situation which now exists in most of those[30] towns which it has been your custom for some years[40] to 'service.' The position certainly appears to be very serious[50] for this business, and as I desire to discover just[60] what has been the cause of this strange loss of[70] business recently, I think perhaps it would be wise for[80] you to come south and to spend some days here[90] with the special purpose of considering possible ways and means[100] of starting a drive of some sort to set the[110] business on its feet again. It seems that the question[120] of selling costs does not cause any difficulty and that[130] our present prices are reasonably satisfactory. Please answer by wire.[140] Yours truly, (142)

" B." Vocabulary for Outline Drill

songs	advise (ce)	snake	folks	splashes
snows	sick	sock	guess	suffer
smokes	sight	spade	kiss	civil
sleeps	single	sponge	nose	observes
noise	skin	spoon	notice	coughs
soft	slow	opposite	slave	puffs
silks	smile	press	succeed	diamonds
caps	space	troops	police	reminders
dozen	spoke	solid	loose	vans
sad	stay	poison	suit	cushions
secures	muscles	sex	task	decisions
skies	councils	smell	desks	exercises
crushes	pencils	soap	springs	guests
speeches	vessels	soup	screws	posters
spots	listens	cheese	chance	spirit
sorry	sincere	seed	dance	thus
basins	sincerely	smooth	cans	
hospitals	excels	excuse	cycles	
costumes	brass	execute	settles	
seat	grass	fix	strikes	

Dictation Practice

(33) Dear Mr. Smithson, At our Council Meeting yesterday evening the[10] question of our Autumn Bazaar was given closer discussion. As[20] you know, we are proposing to run this Bazaar in[30] aid of the new Children's Hospital, and as we wish[40] the Bazaar to have every possible chance of success we[50] are anxious to secure your help. If, for instance, you[60] would kindly consent to open the Bazaar for us, making[70] a suitable speech, we should be exceedingly grateful. We realize[80] that you must receive many requests for

speeches at Prize[90] Givings, Whist Drives, Bazaars, etc., and that you must[100] consequently sometimes find the proceedings rather wearisome; but in spite[110] of this we sincerely hope that you will listen with[120] willing ears to our plea and that you will find[130] it possible to respond. We do not propose to fix[140] the opening date of the Bazaar until we have received[150] an answer from you, but we suggest Wednesday, the sixth[160] of September, as a suitable day. Will you please let[170] us know as early as you can whether you will[180] agree to make the speech for us as requested, and[190] secondly whether the suggested date would be satisfactory for you.[200] With very kind regards and with some apologies for once[210] more seeking your services, We are, Yours sincerely,   (218)

(34) Sally's nose felt cold, and when she lifted her head[10] from the blankets she saw little snow flakes slowly falling.[20] In spring, she thought, one wakes from sleep to hear[30] the soft song of the birds, as they greet the[40] rising sun. Sometimes there is a pause, a moment's sudden[50] silence, and then the concert begins again, with renewed force.[60] One listens in sleepy delight for some minutes and then[70] jumps out of bed, pushes up the sash of the[80] small window and looks out upon the serene scene. The[90] sky is filled with the soft colours of the early[100] morning, splashes of yellow and pink, gold and red, mixing[110] together like the colours on the artist's palette. The chimneys[120] of the two little cottages are already smoking, and a[130] small boy is singing as he feeds the hens. Can[140] one stay longer inside the house on such a morning?[150] One washes hastily, pulls on a simple sleeveless dress and,[160] with costume in hand, runs out through the silky grass[170] to where the stream flows between its high banks. One[180] shivers slightly as one plunges into the sparkling water. Sally[190] sighed. It was pleasant to think of sunny spring days,[200] but this morning it was December, it was cold, and[210] it was snowing. Sometimes, Sally decided as she snuggled beneath[220] the clothes again, spring *can* seem far behind.   (228)

" C." Vocabulary for Outline Drill

misery	canvasser	spruce	selections	signify-ied-icant
facile	Surrey	secretarial	possessions	selfish-ness
Singapore	design	sprints	adjusts	inspect-ed-ion
sneeze	cancer	dispensing	solicitors	discharge-d
cruisers	sanctity	diffidence	sensible-y-ity	executive
licence	smoothly	hunts	certificate	investment
Johnson	confessor	supplementary	expedient	maximum
receipts	Sydney	sever	expediency	minimum
poisonous	Seine	civilized	extinguish-ed	sympathetic
guides	absorbs	civilian	inconsiderate	university
spades	Jackson	archives	subscribe-d	
Snowdon	suddenly	operatives	subscription	
vaseline	Samuel	frowns	substantial-ly	
laughs	intersects	nouns	mathematics	

Dictation Practice

(35) Messrs. Samuel J. Johnson & Sons, 75 Somerset Street,[10] South Streatham. Dear Sirs, Thank you for your cheques in[20] settlement of the two outstanding accounts. We are now enclosing[30] receipts.

Our Mr. Simpson has recently returned from a short[40] visit to Singapore, and he has brought back with him[50] a selection of exquisite Chinese silks, some of which seem[60] to us to be specially suitable for your class of[70] business. We regret that it is not possible for us[80] to send you sample lengths of these silks, but we[90] can say with absolute confidence that it would certainly be[100] worth while to send one of your experts to our[110] Wholesale Depot to inspect the full lengths. They are silks[120] for the connoisseur and are a splendid investment. If you[130] care to suggest a time for such a visit we[140] will arrange to have our Mr. Simpson at the Depot[150] to display the silks. Yours faithfully, (156)

(36) Mr. Suffolk's lips twitched slightly as he sauntered away from[10] the solicitor's office and turned his steps towards Piccadilly Circus.[20] It had once been said of Mr. Suffolk that he[30] was the secretary of one's dreams. He was always spruce[40] and smart, both in his own person and in his[50] work. He was first at his desk in the morning[60] and the last to leave it at night. No piles[70] of unanswered letters littered his tables, no heaps of cigarette[80] ash left their stale smell in his room. He was[90] a facile writer and was always civil and sympathetic towards[100] callers, however tiresome. He spoke to superiors with the maximum[110] of respect but with confidence, and to juniors with a[120] suggestion of distance but with the minimum of condescension. He[130] could be trusted with the firm's most secret facts and[140] figures. The light of loyalty which burned in his eyes[150] was seldom extinguished, and he never questioned the expediency of[160] any course suggested to him by his chiefs. Now, as[170] he was standing on the edge of the pavement waiting[180] to cross the street, a passer-by chancing to gaze idly[190] at him was struck with the look of misery he[200] had surprised upon the countenance of this man, with his[210] smart clothes and polished shoes. He turned and watched Mr.[220] Suffolk for some seconds as he nervously attempted the crossing. (230)

(37) (a) Thomas Sykes is a sensible youth, and thoroughly deserves his[10] many successes, particularly his outstanding achievement of gaining the Higher[20] Certificate for Mathematics. His parents are so anxious to display[30] their appreciation of his achievements that they are making a[40] substantial subscription to your Fund for taking a selection of[50] the senior boys to Athens. As the selected boys are[60] certain to have all sorts of significant and marvellous experiences[70]

on their journey it would be selfish and inconsiderate of[80] parents
not to discharge their responsibility in this respect by[90] subscribing
suitably.   (92)

(*b*) luxurious inexpedient salubrious sanctimonious syndicates fiscal
scandalous salutary cognizance Cincinnati convalescent incendiarism
supersede subtlety sophisticated spectroscope skirmish

PART TWO: Strokes eSS and Zee

" A." Vocabulary for Outline Drill

ease	asks	science	sizes	see
easy	asked	sciences	sizing	sees
easily	issue	scientist	say	seaside
easiness	issued	scientific	says	continuous
uneasy	issuing	unscientific	so	was
ask	issues	size	also	whose

Dictation Practice

(38) Thank you so much for sending us the information regarding[10]
the size of your advertisement which is to appear in[20] this month's
issue of *Science for Young People*. The different[30] sizes of the advertisements for this issue have made it[40] less easy than usual for us
to see to the[50] make-up. When writing to you I ought also to have[60]
asked you if you desire the advertisement to appear in[70] the August
and September issues in addition to the July[80] issue. Continuous
running for such advertisements often brings good results.[90] So
long as I have this information within the next[100] two weeks it will
be in good time for the[110] August issue. We have an uneasy feeling
that the paper[120] *Science for Young People* is not reaching so many
homes[130] as we could wish, and we have under consideration the[140]
issue of a new paper called *Scientific Facts for the*[150] *Unscientific
Person*, but we are not yet able to say[160] just what size or form such
a paper would take.   (170)

(39) I am writing to say that my mother has asked[10] me to find
out whether you could come with us[20] to the seaside at the end of
this month. I[30] am also writing to May, asking her the same thing.[40]
We have taken a house at South Sea for a[50] month. It is called *Sea
View*, and while it is[60] not of remarkable size there would be enough
room for[70] you, if only you will say ' yes,' as I hope[80] so much you will.
I am sure that you can[90] easily get away at this time of the year. (99)

" B." Vocabulary for Outline Drill

zoo	assist	cease	policy	process
Zulu	sister	ceaseless	disease	sighs
zinc	assessment	sausages	society	especial-ly
zeal	sciatica	scissors	joyous	establish-ed-ment
ice	sawdust	juicy	possess	
escape	sawmill	crazy	possesses	
essay	lazy	sauce	acid	
Mrs.	busy	saucy	acids	

Dictation Practice

(40) The attack of sciatica had left Jessie feeling very lazy,[10] and this laziness presented little Lizzie with a splendid chance[20] to go into the village alone. She was quick to[30] seize her opportunity. She tried not to show how joyous[40] she felt, and followed the policy of professing readiness to[50] assist Jessie in every way possible. Lizzie possessed a saucy[60] cheery little face, and all the shop assistants were pleased[70] to see her, even when she kicked her feet so[80] that the sawdust so carefully sprinkled on the floors shot[90] up in clouds behind her. She loved best of all[100] to visit the General Stores, where such things as sausages,[110] saucers, scissors, acid drops, asbestos mats, zinc baths of different[120] sizes, and pictures of the animals at the zoo, were[130] grouped together in crazy friendship. The crowded counters filled Lizzie's[140] mind with ceaseless wonder and her heart with joyous happiness.[150] When the assistants were too busy to talk to her[160] she would roam slowly round the shop, her eyes missing[170] not the slightest detail.

It was always with a little[180] sigh that Lizzie eventually left the shop and the kind[190] assistants, and returned slowly home to Jessie, whose continual complaints[200] about sciatica made poor little Lizzie sigh still more deeply. (210)

" C." Vocabulary for Outline Drill

zero	Australia	seasonal	agency	bankruptcy
zealous	seagull	Maizie	pursue	suspect-ed
zone	suicide	fancy	decease	esquire
zones	societies	Nancy	disease	enthusiasm-tic
Osborne	sewer	contemptuous	ingenious	
Austria	Oscar	excise	ingeniously	
astonish	Suez	precise	ingenuous	
auspices	season	recess	ingenuously	

Dictation Practice

(41) Dear Mr. Oscar, You will have heard of the sad[10] decease of Edward Osborne, Esq., while on his visit to[20] Austria, a visit made in the attempt to effect a[30] cure for an obscure disease of the eyes. Mr. Osborne[40] had the sole agency for us in the zone marked[50] on the attached sketch. We know you to be an[60] enthusiastic supporter of our goods, and we are certain that[70] if we could persuade you to accept the agency you[80] would pursue a policy satisfactory to us. So far as[90] the precise details of such an agency are concerned, these[100] could be discussed after ascertaining that you are willing[110] to consider this offer. As our busy season will commence[120] shortly, please let us have an early reply. In the[130] meantime, kindly treat the matter as one of secrecy. Yours[140] sincerely, (141)

(42) (a) Precise details of the suggested sewage scheme have not been[10] circulated, but the enthusiasm shown by Mr. Cecil in these[20]

preliminary stages is easy to understand, especially when it is[30] remembered that in the event of the adoption of the[40] scheme the Cecil firm would certainly receive the contract for[50] the execution of the work and would thereby be rescued[60] from a state which, so to speak, at present borders[70] upon bankruptcy. (72)

(b) eschew exiguous vacuous secede cessation ecstasy assiduous foresee fatuous astrology ascetic isosceles

SECTION FIVE: CIRCLES SWay AND SeZ
PART ONE: Circle SWay
" A." Vocabulary for Outline Drill

sweet	to	on	should	much
sweetness	all	but	can	which
sweetest	two, too	he	come	put
sweeter	together	who	go	it
of	altogether	and	give-n	

Dictation Practice

(43) "Friendship makes even water sweet." So runs an old saying.[10] As we know only too well, most people have a[20] strong desire for sweet foods and indeed for the sweet[30] things of life generally. In times of peace, there is[40] no reason why people should not have as much sweet[50] food as they desire provided, of course, that they do[60] not go beyond the limits of what is good for[70] their bodily health. There is no reason why they should[80] not as well take as much of the sweetness of[90] life as they can, provided again that they do not[100] go beyond what is good for themselves and provided that,[110] by taking sweetness for themselves, they do not make life[120] less sweet for those whom they meet and influence. In[130] times of war, however, many of the sweet things of[140] life are put beyond our reach, and often as a[150] result they seem to our eyes even sweeter and more[160] to be desired.

Sweet, by the way, is a word[170] which is worked very hard. We say that certain food[180] is sweet, that a child looks sweet, that a voice[190] sounds sweet. We use expressions such as "You grow sweeter[200] as the years go by" and "The sweetest girl in[210] the world." Ought we not to try to express our[220] meaning a little more clearly in these different cases, limiting[230] the use of the word *sweet* only to those cases[240] where it may be rightly used?   (246)

" B." Vocabulary for Outline Drill

swim	swan	swells	swears	sweep
swam	switch	swol en	suite	sweeper
swum	swept	swelling	Swindon	
swing	swallow	swear	swagger	

Dictation Practice

(44) Messrs. Swan and Selby, 19 Swings Road, Swindon. Gentlemen, Thank[10] you for the details of your new Swindon Electric Sweeper.[20] As we trust that it may be possible for us[30] to take on the sale of this new sweeper, we[40] shall be pleased to accept your offer of a special[50] visit from your Mr. Swan. We suggest that he calls[60] one morning about 11 o'clock. Yours truly,   (67)

(45) As we are all aware, it is a very old[10] custom to use homing pigeons to carry messages, and most[20] of us have sometimes seen a pigeon sweeping gracefully through[30] the air, its little heart no doubt swelling with the[40] pride of its importance. But many less famous birds share[50] the homing sense of the pigeon, and among these birds[60] is the swallow. The swallow has inspired many a poet[70] to write lines to it as it swoops low over[80] the water in the sunshine. The swallow which we watch[90] in summer may have spent the winter in some far-off[100] country before returning here to delight our eyes during the[110] warmer days of spring and summer. Careful experiments have been[120] carried out with sea-swallows. Selected birds have been carefully[130] marked and taken away on board a vessel for a[140] distance of from 500 to 800 miles. At[150] a chosen point the sea-swallows have been set free,[160] and most of them have been seen again less than[170] a week afterwards at their original home. As we know,[180] many animals have this homing sense highly developed.

(188)

" C." Vocabulary for Outline Drill

swamp	swivel	swarm	Swansea	swaying
swelter	Swiss	sward	Sweden	persuaded
swifter	Swanson	swerve	Switzerland	
swindle	swansdown	swerved	sway	

Dictation Practice

(46) It was a day of sweltering heat, and we sat[10] almost without movement on the soft sward near the house,[20] watching the mist which hovered over the swampy ground in[30] the distance. Swanson kept swearing gently at our enforced idleness,[40] but on the whole we kept our tempers as well[50] as could be expected. The air seemed to swim with[60] the heat, and we had no energy for violence. All[70] the same, Swanson switched back to his main theme with[80] monotonous repetition. "It is a swindle, absolutely. I do not[90] believe this is an accident. If persuasion was no use[100] we should have used force and swept them all from[110] our path." But even as he said it he seemed[120] almost to swoon with fatigue, and all his usual swagger[130] had left him. A great swarm of insects droned overhead,[140] occasionally swooping towards us as if purposely to annoy.   (149)

(47) (a) It took countless hours of unceasing persuasion to sway the[10] Swedish soldier from his reiterated intention of attempting to cross[20] into Switzerland by scaling the Alps at a particularly difficult[30] section, dropping down on the Swiss side where there was[40] little probability of a frontier barrier. Once we had persuaded[50] him to swerve from his hazardous plan we took swift[60] action.   (61)

(b) suavity swathed Swedenborgian swindle swineherd St. Swithin Swanage swirling dissuasive

PART TWO: Circle SeZ

"A." Vocabulary for Outline Drill

services	taxes	basis	themselves	for
losses	businesses	bases	ourselves	have
expresses	success	exist	be	thank-ed
forces	successes	exists	to be	think
senses	successful	sizes	had	
pleases	successfully	distances	do	
causes	necessary	experiences	different	
uses	necessarily	insurances	large	

Dictation Practice

(48) It is seen clearly that businesses which have been in[10] existence for many years and which, as is shown from[20] yearly reports, have had good sales experiences, are now showing[30] signs of being much less successful and in some cases[40] are even facing serious losses. This has been taking place[50] all over the country. Many causes are put forward by[60] the businesses themselves. Heavier taxes and the higher rates[70] for insurances are among the causes. Other causes are increased[80] costs of road services and increased rates of pay to[90] employees made necessary by the higher cost of living. The[100] head of a well-known organization, with offices all over the[110] country, expresses the view that the Government will have necessarily[120] to take measures to put prices on a sure basis[130] as soon as such steps can be taken.   (138)

(49) He announces to-day that a number of special courses on[10] different sciences are to be offered in the school this[20] year. These courses are to cover as wide a field[30] as is possible, and the purposes and uses of each[40] talk will be fully set out in the time-table.[50] As soon as this is ready it is probable that[60] we shall be asked to offer our services in connection[70] with the courses, perhaps on the basis of delivering two[80] talks a week for 12 weeks. If so, I think[90] we should agree to do this.   (96)

"B." Vocabulary for Outline Drill

addresses	praises	invoices	exercise	chances
chooses	races	loses	exercises	princes
classes	supposes	noises	exercised	glances
closes	advises	refuses	insist	policies
glasses	ceases	necessity	dances	

Dictation Practice

(50) Lacey's General Stores, 3 Princes Street, Swansea.
Gentlemen, We are[10] enclosing invoices for the various goods which you have received[20] from us during the past quarter, and we regret to[30] add that we find ourselves on this occasion under the[40] necessity of exercising our right to demand payment within fourteen[50] days

from the date given on the invoices. As you[60] know, we very seldom exercise this right but the difficulty[70] of the present situation places us in a position where[89] it is not possible to follow our usual policies of[90] serving the interests of both buyer and manufacturer. We have[100] indeed received two advices from the manufacturer in this city[110] in which he presses for cash payments from us, stating[120] that in future his firm refuses to take chances on[130] delayed payments. We in our turn must insist upon prompt[140] payment. We trust you will understand the difficult position in[150] which this places us. Assuring you of our best services,[160] We are, Yours truly,   (164)

(51) According to this statement, if Daisy chooses to attend these[10] classes to learn old country dances she will be given[20] very good chances for expert stage training. Miss Lucy's letter[30] praises Daisy's abilities, and stresses that she possesses everything that[40] is a necessity for a successful career on the stage.[50] As Daisy herself persists in her wish to attend the[60] classes it would probably be unfair for her parents to[70] exercise their possessive rights and resist her wishes.   (78)

" C." Vocabulary for Outline Drill

convinces	allowances	emphasizes	axis	process
commences	phases	emphasized	Mississippi	excess
economizes	incessant	phthisis	Ulysses	access
suppresses	possessive	census	entrances	criticize
induces	successor	exhausting	condenses	fallacies
rejoices	emphasize	decisive	ensconses	jealousies

Dictation Practice

(52) Most of the speeches emphasized the necessity for the granting[10] of these licences. In such cases, however, one of the[20] principal difficulties arises from the speaker who is known to[30] have access to necessary facts but who, aware of local[40] jealousies, deliberately suppresses valuable information and criticizes certain people to[50] excess. Fortunately, this type of speaker generally induces a feeling[60] of criticism of his methods among the more alert of[70] his hearers, and frequently convinces them that it is their[80] duty to oppose him. Although therefore two most prominent citizens[90] made exhaustive and exhausting speeches against the granting of the[100] licences, it was decided by vote that it was in[110] the public interest to licence the two halls for the[120] holding of dances and concerts, subject to certain very definite[130] conditions being complied with.   (134)

(53) (a) It is said that the collector of interesting pieces of[10] glass rejoices in seizing any chances that present themselves to[20] possess

specimens of genuine 17th century glasses. He eulogizes the[30] glasses to all his acquaintances, and his analysis tends to[40] prove that most of these glasses were either made by[50] Venetians or under direct Venetian influences. Emphasis is also placed[60] on the rarity of 18th century cider glasses.   (68)

(*b*) synopsis synthesis ruses diagnosis parenthesis amanuensis abscesses indices

SECTION SIX: LOOPS STee AND STeR
PART ONE: Loop STee
"A." Vocabulary for Outline Drill

state	just	housed	distanced	in, any
stop	priced	rest	cost	own
stone	lost	wastes	caused	me
steel	taxed	costs	first	him
still	test	suggestion	most	shall
store	list	artistic	influenced	wish
west	faced	stopper	next	
August	announced	experienced	though	
best	forced	cleansed	them	

Dictation Practice

(54) On the first of August last it was announced by[10] the Authorities that they have been forced to stop all[20] new house building in this city during the rest of[30] this year. According to their statement, they have been influenced[40] by the fact that they are faced with a shortage[50] of labour, having lost many of their regular workers, and[60] difficulty is being experienced in the delivery of steel and[70] other necessary materials. Further, costs have increased heavily in many[80] directions. Work, however, is still to go on in[90] the case of houses already being built, and in this[100] connection it is satisfactory to note that the houses at[110] West End, which have been planned on such modern and[120] artistic lines, are to be completed.

It was also announced[130] by the Authorities that no further names will be added[140] to the list of those requiring houses. While the statement[150] at first caused a certain amount of regret among those[160] citizens who had hoped shortly to be housed in new[170] quarters, there is no suggestion from any of the people[180] that the action of the Authorities is not just. Neither[190] has there been any suggestion that the Authorities should have[200] acted otherwise or taken steps to improve the general position.   (210)

" B." Vocabulary for Outline Drill

stamp	style	forest	steady	stagger
steam	coast	tastes	stitch	danced
staff	honest	mixed	stem	contrasted
stage	post	chest	stocking	upset
stick	advised	digestion	stomach	tested
stocks	beast	disgust	vast	honesty
star	breakfast	mist	sticky	
storm	nest	paste	stiff	
study	stood	protest	steeper	

Dictation Practice

(55) Jeffrey Stubbs, Esq., 14 Star Road, Stepney.
Dear Mr. Stubbs,[10] You may be surprised to learn that we have been[20] advised that we have now reached the stage when an[30]

addition to our Stores is practically forced upon us. To[40] be honest, we must admit that we take this advice[50] with slightly mixed feelings, as we know only too well[60] that the present is not the best time to make[70] vast extensions, in view of the increased cost of materials,[80] particularly of steel and stone. It is remarkable, however, that[90] contrasted with the conditions experienced by many firms, these Stores[100] have experienced a steeper rise in profits recently than for[110] some years past, and a study of the figures has[120] convinced us that we must go ahead. As your branch[130] of the Stores will be influenced by the extensions, may[140] we suggest that in the first place you call here[150] on Thursday next when we can put before you our[160] plans, and you can make any suggestions or protests which[170] you feel can, with honesty, be justified. We would like[180] you to bring with you exact figures of the stocks[190] held by you at the end of August, and a[200] complete list of your staff, with ages and experience. Such[210] a list may help us to form some idea as[220] to how many of the trained staff are likely to[230] stick by us during the next few months. Also, it[240] is most important at this stage that we look carefully[250] into the matter of general costs, and take all possible[260] steps to stop waste where it can be traced.

We[270] await receipt of confirmation that you will call on Thursday[280] next. Yours sincerely,   (283)

(56) Box ST 124, *The Morning Star*, Strand[10] House, London, S.E.10

Sir,   *Advertisement for Shorthand-Typist*[20]

In reply to your advertisement for an experienced shorthand-typist,[30] which appeared in yesterday's issue of *The Morning Star*, I[40] herewith apply to be considered for the post.

I am[50] an experienced shorthand writer, having for the past two years[60] held a post on the staff of Messrs. Guest and[70] Stephens, Stockbrokers. The post is one which involves the reporting[80] and typing of the Minutes of special meetings, and much[90] of my work has been done on my own responsibility,[100] without being supervised by seniors. I am also used to[110] doing work of a very confidential nature.

I have passed[120] the tests of the principal Examination Bodies of the country[130] for shorthand and typewriting, my speeds being 160[140] and 85 words a minute respectively. I gained a[150] special "Distinction" mark in the advanced tests for shorthand and[160] typewriting held by the State Examining Body.

My present employers[170] know of my desire to obtain a new post, and[180] have expressed their willingness to testify to my abilities.

I[190] trust that my application will receive your consideration. Yours faithfully,   (200)

" C." Vocabulary for Outline Drill

stag	opposed	stampede	stoker	distinguish-ed
Stirling	subsidized	testify	glanced	distinguishes
stainless	chemists	justifiable	enhanced	distinguishing
stigmatize	diffused	statistics	bronzed	distinguishable
Stephen	amethyst	statistical	deceit	
stimulus	statue	scholastic	gazette	
stealthy	statute	stupor	distinction	
Stanford	stenography	stutter	distinct	

Dictation Practice

(57) One of our most distinguished writers to-day is Henry Williamson.[10] His stories of animal life, his books of natural history,[20] and his novels, all bear the stamp of the artist.[30] The thrilling interest of what he writes is enhanced by[40] the scholastic style which distinguishes his writing and which makes[50] his books outstanding as literature as well as sources of[60] information. Those whose hearts beat fast when they are lucky[70] enough to spy a wild deer standing like a statue[80] on the skyline of some solitary hill will probably already[90] have read the book *Story of a Red Deer*, by[100] Sir John Fortescue. Their tastes will lead them, too, to[110] read *The Old Stag*, by Henry Williamson, a more recent[120] publication. It is a series of animal stories, and the[130] first is the story of a stag called Stumberleap. We[140] are introduced to him as he fights in the wind[150] and the rain with another stag. The two stags thrust[160] and stab and plunge, each trying desperately to wrest an[170] advantage from the other. Antlers clash again, and a young[180] hind steals from the herd to butt the enemy in[190] the flank. They seem lost in the battle, but suddenly[200] they stop. Their nostrils have caught the scent of man,[210] and they are away. But Stumberleap is born to fight,[220] and his next adventure is to be chased by man[230] and dogs. He was made of lasting stuff, however, and[240] he puts up a fight for his existence which sends[250] many a hound staggering back to his kennel less confidently[260] than he had left it.

(265)

(58) (a) Two books which would be of the greatest interest to[10] anyone fascinated by the vast expanse and unsurpassed glory of[20] a brilliant night sky are *The Story of the Stars*[30] and *In Starry Realms*. Those of more advanced tastes are[40] advised to read *The Mysterious Universe*. In the latter book[50] we are informed on the first page that the total[60] number of stars in the universe is probably something like[70] the total number of grains of sand on all the[80] seashores of the world. A very short study of the[90] science of the stars reveals an extent of time and[100] space which is almost beyond imagination. In these modern days[110] any simple book on astronomy will teach us about fixed[120] stars, double stars, variable stars, star clusters, and so on.[130] The first simple maps of the principal

constellations were made[140] thousands of years ago, but until the mastery of the[150] telescope knowledge progressed slowly although steadily. For the most part,[160] the mysterious universe was indeed wrapped in mystery; but man's[170] thirst for knowledge was always growing, and the invention and[180] rapid improvement of the telescope proved an immense stimulus to[190] endeavour and study. Astronomers forecast with astonishing accuracy the smallest[200] events of the heavens years in advance of the actual[210] happening.

(211)

(*b*) analyst oculist staccato statuette static bombast stagnant unbiassed stenographer stethoscope stigmatizing stentorian stipendiary statistician stampeded stadium fantastic

PART TWO: Loop STeR

"A." Vocabulary for Outline Drill

master	masterpieces	youngster	language, owing	important-ce
masters	waster	westerly	thing	improve-d-ment
mastering	wasters	mastered	young	
masterpiece	taster	mastery	usual-ly	

Dictation Practice

(59) Probably all of you have at some time been to[10] a National Picture Show to see the masterpieces painted by[20] the Old Masters of the past. In many cases you[30] will have read something about the work of one of[40] these Old Masters, and you will expect to see something[50] very wonderful. But when you come face to face with[60] the pictures you sometimes find it difficult to understand why[70] these paintings, in which the colours are no longer clear[80] and in which the subjects seem so strange and heavy,[90] should be considered masterpieces. But at other times you look[100] at the work of a great master with real respect,[110] able to value the masterly touch. Noting the clear colours[120] of the oils, you ask yourself how these colours have[130] come to last so long in such a clear state.[140] It is said that some of these Old Masters knew[150] some special point about the making up of oil colours[160] which was afterwards lost and which no one has since[170] discovered. Whether or not this is true, it is certainly[180] a fact that the colours on some of these old[190] masterpieces have kept new and clear while others have not.[200] One of the very best known of the great masters[210] of the past is said to have been so mean[220] that he would not spend much money on his paints,[230] and owing to this meanness the paints he worked with[240] were of poor quality and the colours on his pictures[250] are no longer clear, with the result that his work[260] has lost much of its value and importance.

(268)

" B." Vocabulary for Outline Drill

duster	faster	lustre	Leicester	pastry
dusters	investor	coaster	Dunster	mystery
poster	Westminster	administer	plaster	
Chester	Manchester	Webster	restore	

Dictation Practice

(60) I am sure my fellow-investors will agree that the[10] report which has been presented to us to-day is highly[20] satisfactory and is one which will restore confidence in our[30] undertaking throughout the entire country. The Press campaign against the[40] Westminster Poster Agency has been a great mystery to us[50] all, but the facts which have been put before us[60] by Mr. Webster this afternoon explain much that was worrying[70] us. I can say on behalf of all of us[80] here that we have absolute faith in those who administer[90] the affairs of the Agency. It was natural that there[100] should be some falling off in poster advertising during the[110] autumn of last year, particularly in the case of cinema[120] posters, and I do not think that any explanation is[130] required regarding this falling-off.

There is, however, one point[140] which bothers me, and no doubt bothers some of my[150] fellow-investors also, and that is the persistent and public[160] claim made by the Manchester and London Poster Agency that[170] they can show by facts and figures that they get[180] faster results through their poster advertising than any other agency.[190] Have any steps been taken by the Board to verify[200] this statement? If not, does the Chairman believe that the[210] statement can be verified? I ask that it be put[220] on record that we in this company voice our strong[230] disapproval of such statements.

Finally, I wish to express the[240] thanks of those present to-day to both the Chairman and[250] Mr. Webster for their hard work on our behalf.   (259)

" C." Vocabulary for Outline Drill

register	Lobsters	pastor	Chesterfield	gesture
registers	Lister	jester	muster	pasture
roadster	foster	gangster	cloisters	chemistry
upholster	Lancaster	Doncaster	spinster	registry
upholsterer	sinister	costers	spinsters	

Dictation Practice

(61) The whereabouts of the car remain a mystery. In the[10] register of missing cars it is stated that the gangsters[20] were last seen jumping into a smart black roadster, upholstered[30] in red leather. The registration number of the roadster was[40] TA74, and the gangsters headed in the[50] direction of Doncaster. A private car chased them, but the[60] roadster was the faster car and was soon lost to[70] sight. It is thought that the gangsters abandoned the roadster[80] in a pastoral lane.   (84)

(62) (*a*) Mr. Baxter emphasized that he wished to register his profound[10] dissatisfaction. It was imperative that they moved much faster if[20] they were to keep pace with other manufacturers. In these[30] sinister times we were urged to muster all our forces,[40] and not only to foster existing industries but to create[50] new ones. The extraordinary demand for construction materials offered a[60] marvellous opportunity to makers of plastics. They must bestir themselves.[70] There was already on the market a plastic declared to[80] be blister-proof. A cigarette left burning on a table[90] made of this new plastic would not singe or blister[100] the surface, nor would it leave a mark of any[110] kind. If we ourselves do not move faster we shall[120] find that we have been left behind in the struggle. (130)

(*b*) ancestors forester barristers consternation adjuster lustre impostors palmistry dextrous

SECTION SEVEN: VOWELS, DIPHTHONGS, TRIPHONES, AND DIPHONES

"A." Vocabulary for Outline Drill

authority	boyish	either	bases	why
experience	existed	record	position	I, eye
memory	question	necessary	saying	January
easily	distribution	observations	engineer	February
babies	directly	political	a, an	never, November
animal	history	activity	the	manufacture
lower	taxation	education	O! oh! owe	knowledge
bodily	children	details	ought, aught, awe	acknowledge
serious	weighing	announcing	how	
winter	milk	indeed	you	

Dictation Practice

(63) A big part of what we know about the life[10] led by the people who lived in past ages has[20] been got from records, the existence of which was not[30] discovered for many hundreds of years. These records were written[40] on stone, on paper, and on other materials, and from[50] them experts have built up, piece by piece, an almost[60] complete picture of life during the earlier ages of man's[70] existence upon earth. We can now read the story of[80] the lives of people who lived perhaps a thousand, two[90] thousand, or three thousand years ago. We know something about[100] their political ideas, their views upon educational systems, how they[110] first set about farming the land, the first use they[120] made of stone and iron, and other natural materials, and[130] how their knowledge of engineering grew. We can learn from[140] books the sort of food liked by the people of[150] past ages, the value placed upon family life, and the[160] position of the children in relation to the family as[170] a whole. We can find information regarding their methods of[180] taxation, the size of their early cities, the animals brought[190] into the service of man, the power of the people[200] to provide for their growing requirements, and the first early[210] steps forward in their knowledge of science.

(217)

(64) Mr. W. Turner, 15 West End Drive, North Wells.

Dear[10] Mr. Turner, It must seem to you that I have[20] been a very long time answering your kind letter of[30] the third April. I regret to have left your letter[40] over for so long, but the fact is that a[50] great part of my time has been taken up with[60] the planning of some important new work for the War[70] Office which has recently been put into our hands. This[80] work is now in operation, however, and I have this[90] week been in a position to give some consideration and[100] attention to your suggestions. In the first place, I must[110] express to you my personal thanks, and the thanks of[120] the other members of the Board, for your kindness in[130] offering us your valuable and experienced help, and in placing[140] before us a suggested new plan of operation for our[150] control work. It is true that some change in the[160] method of control has been necessary for some little time[170] past. I have therefore carefully tested your suggestions from several[180] points of view, and I have been forced to the[190] belief that they are reasonable and workable. Naturally, it would[200] be necessary to see the plans in much more detailed[210] form before any final agreement could be come to.

One[220] important fact is that the carrying out of the suggestions[230] would mean several rather wide changes in certain points of[240] our works organization, and there are several difficulties in the[250] way of making such changes at the present moment.

I[260] think the next step to take is for you to[270] call and see me personally, and I suggest either Tuesday[280] morning or Thursday morning of next week, when I shall[290] be free to see you. Please let us know if[300] either of these dates is all right for you. Yours[310] very truly,   (312)

" B." Vocabulary for Outline Drill

America	bath	match	pa	oak
normal	bit	belong	pack	ma
camera	enemy	tongue	boots	papa
envelope	parcels	tooth	period	map
bottom	box	son, sun	pick	dog
attacking	musician	community	tall	monkey
loudly	jewels	affect	tea	fee
aim	bite	bag	thee	feed
attach	comb	yellow	thou	funny
nice	cow	ideal	pig	kick
immense	aids	package	tie	tail
mouth	comparison	cup	toe	key
quietly	fowl	inch	knee	bow
billion	damage	path	neck	choice
famously	violent	thick	manage	cooks
chalking	ball	votes	game	county
drawer	eggs	beg	gate	debt
musical	camp	bills	item	death
cruel	bell	type	job	edge
bays	top	village	kid	canvas
bee	cake	visit	kill	ink
beat	carriage	apparatus	unto	loyal
allow	avenue	dirty	thumb	

Dictation Practice

(65) Gentlemen, In response to your request, we are enclosing three[10] packages of our high-grade China Tea. All our blends[20] are selected from teas taken from the finest tea-growing[30] areas of China, a fact which needs no emphasis. The[40] qualities of tea contained in the pink and the purple[50] packets are of a pleasing and refreshing fragrance and are[60] popular among those whose tastes are not fully mature. In[70] the yellow packet is a tea of a

superior quality,[80] with a flavour and perfume appreciated by the trained tea-[90]drinker. We keep a plentiful stock of these three blends[100] and can supply upon demand. When purchasing you should watch[110] for the distinguishing trade mark on the attractive tea containers[120] in which the blends are packed. Beware of cheap imitations[130] which will only disappoint in the long run. Should you[140] be interested in more rare qualities of China teas, we[150] can send you a number of tiny parcels containing enough[160] tea of different varieties to make four cups of the[170] exact strength advisable. It is desirable to order these more[180] expensive teas definitely in advance of customers' requirements, as we[190] do not keep large stocks of the more rare qualities.[200] Yours truly, (202)

(66) Most children delight in reading tales about animals, and there[10] is an immense amount of literature at their disposal. The aunt[20] who is aware of an approaching birthday and who wishes[30] to find a gift which will be really appreciated can[40] make no better choice than a copy of *Red Fox*,[50] by Charles G. D. Roberts. This book is described as[60] the story of the fox's adventures in the Canadian backwoods[70] and his final triumph over the enemies of his kind.[80] Red Fox was always willing to bare his teeth and[90] fight every inch of the way. He was strong enough[100] and brave enough to be a match for anything which[110] dared to attack him or cause him annoyance. All the[120] exciting incidents recorded are, the author assures us, in keeping[130] with the known capacities and abilities of the fox family,[140] and the incidents described make a fascinating study. (148)

" G." Vocabulary for Outline Drill

territorial	diets	conveyances	automatic	accede
sawing	China	caution	lecture	exceed
elicit	Dardanelles	cruelty	Winnipeg	ah !
preoccupation	empower	questionnaire	estimate	aye, eh?
lucidity	casually	incurred	India	acknowledgment
incapacitate	municipal	insistence	co-operative	peculiar-ity
desultory	peeping	militarism	Newcastle	familiar-ity
statistician	indecision	philosophy	paragraph	familiarize
aerial	parallel	indebted	adopt	uniform-ity-ly
collaboration	decisive	immensely	adapt	unanimous-ly
rapidity	crocus	loyalty	amazement	
felicity	pacify	occurrence	amusement	
modesty	luminous	Adelaide	amazing	
sour	rejoicing	kicking	amusing	

Dictation Practice

(67) Old Lucas had grown lazy with the passage of the[10] years. His estate, starting from a few humble acres, was[20] now a vast piece of territory. He had a staff[30] of competent, industrious men, loyal and able to act rapidly[40] and decisively when the occasion necessitated quick action. Success had[50] softened old Lucas, and

his round on horseback had become[60] an automatic and casual routine. He no longer glanced to[70] left and right with the alert pride of the big[80] estate-owner. He found the afternoon warm and sultry, he[90] was pre-occupied, and was indeed finding it difficult to resist[100] the temptation to dismount and rest for a time among[110] the line of trees which ran almost parallel with the[120] sluggish river. He patted his horse's head in a desultory,[130] absent-minded manner, and moved unheeding past the broken fence.   (140)

(68) Imagine, if you will, days of severe frost, with temperatures[10] dropping to below zero. Snow is piled high on road[20] and railway, bringing normal services to a standstill and leaving[30] people in town and country without adequate supplies of such[40] commodities as milk and coal. Lorries and railway engines are[50] buried deep in snow-drifts, and it takes the strenuous[60] work of many men to dig them out and release[70] the drivers. Imagine, too, the necessity for food being dropped[80] from aeroplanes to people marooned in the villages below, villages[90] only a few miles apart but for the time completely[100] isolated. Families wake up in the morning to find water-[110]pipes solid. The casual lighting of a fire causes a[120] boiler to burst, bringing down the side of a house[130] and injuring the occupants. Cement paths, laid out with pride[140] in the summer, crack until they resemble crazy paving, and[150] odd bricks in the garden wall crumble like powder. People[160] whose duty unfortunately forces them to brave the elements outside[170] pick their way slowly through piles of slippery snow, or[180] grope along close to railings and walls as they peer[190] through the fog. They have thick scarves tied round their[200] heads to prevent their ears from being chilled or frost-[210]bitten. Imagine all this and ask, "Where did it occur?[220] In Russia, perhaps, or Canada, or Norway?" No, it happened[230] here in England where the climate is so "equable."
          (239)

(69) encyclopaedia sanatorium aerated elusory nullifying scholasticism exorbitant aluminium prevaricate Fahrenheit counterfeit miniature pernicious chimneys fulfilled turbulence earnest rehabilitation evacuating irritable preponderating subordinate Mediterranean pre-occupied perseverance immigrant perpetual illuminating erratic depreciation necessitous conscientiously negotiation

SECTION EIGHT: HALVING

PART ONE: Halving of Straight Strokes

" A." Vocabulary for Outline Drill

act	indeed	between	sort	particular
complete	credit	capital	body	opportunity
beds	account	certain	get	build-ing
good	behind	country	painted	told
straight	beautiful	direct	grounded	tried
waits	paint	October	credited	trade, toward
heat	plants	perfect	dated	accord-ing
connect	round	political	doubts	cold, equalled
about	frequent	hundred	rates	gentleman
doubt	spent	regard	quite	gentlemen
bread	want	reports	could	

Dictation Practice

(70) The Secretary, Direct Building Company,
     17 Bread Street, E.C.[10]2.

Dear Sir, I regret to see from your letter[20] that you are doubtful about my position. I do not[30] know how reports of this sort are put round, but[40] you may be quite certain that any doubts you have[50] about the subject are without basis. There is no doubt[60] whatever about my being in a satisfactory position to complete[70] the business between us by the date agreed upon. If[80] you cared to get into direct touch with the bank[90] they could inform you that, although I have perhaps spent[100] larger sums than is usual for me and have called[110] upon my capital more frequently and to a greater degree[120] than is my custom, there is still a larger amount[130] of capital to my credit than is needed to pay[140] your final account. Indeed, between now and October, when according[150] to your statement you expect the building to be complete,[160] large sums amounting to several hundreds of pounds will be[170] credited to my account by businesses with whom I trade[180] regularly but who wait until September of each year to[190] complete payment of accounts. If you still doubt my position,[200] act upon the suggestion given above and go direct to[210] the bank. Yours truly,   (214)

" B." Vocabulary for Outline Drill

blood	exactly	obtained	guide	cloud
cat	skirts	dead	instead	raid
wet	engaged	bend	insects	boats
deeds	bombard	rained	memorandum	goats
coat	output	occurred	patriot	droughts
coats	caught	settled	potato	rats
accept	tickets	spotted	practical	rod
accepted	pots	current	protect	roots
actual	achieved	bucket	tight	commanded
attached	glad	delicate	taught	dotted
catalogue	gladly	secret	cute, queued	acute
includes	height	secretary	proud	treated
decided	heights	democrat	God	
decidedly	basket	grade	pretty	
exact	obliged	grant	duty	

Dictation Practice

(71) All the children were greatly attached to Jet, the shiny[10] black cat. He had achieved his name as a kitten,[20] for as he lay in his basket the spotless coat[30] had settled the matter without any of the heated argument[40] which usually attends such christenings. On the spot it had[50] been decided by all that the name Jet suited him[60] exactly. Jet was a pretty and lively kitten, and he[70] grew into a heavy and pampered cat whose good deeds[80] and misdeeds were talked about and commented upon by the[90] youngsters in all the neighbouring cottages; for Jet had a[100] personality which was accepted as naturally as the personality of[110] a child is accepted. He showed greed for the good[120] things of life, but above all he loved ice cream,[130] and on warm days there was always one child ready[140] to spend his penny on a wafer for the cat.[150] Jet would lick it delicately with his tongue, and when[160] it was finished would make certain that his long whiskers[170] were wiped quite clean. On this particular morning the street[180] was deserted; there were no children and therefore there was[190] no ice cream, for it had rained steadily for several[200] hours, and the roads were very wet. As Jet slipped[210] back into the dryness of the kitchen the wet dripped[220] from his thick and bedraggled coat, and the soft pads[230] of his feet clearly marked his course across the floor.[240] In the corner a bucket was perched on a stool.[250] Jet had been taught by many a sharp lesson that[260] buckets and pots and pans must not be touched; but[270] he was tempted. He walked delicately all round the bucket,[280] and his nose told him that the contents were good.[290] He lifted his front paws on to the edge of[300] the bucket and peeped in. The kitchen was very quiet,[310] and Jet's nose and tongue went straight into the frothy[320] cream. Engaged in this most delightful occupation he was less[330] alert than usual and did not hear Spot, the hated[340] dog, as it entered the kitchen and stole up behind[350] him. (351)

(72) You will be interested to know what has occurred in[10] this connection since our last meeting. Several days ago I[20] received a memorandum from the secretary of the Institute of[30] Democrats and Patriots in which he offered us a substantial[40] grant towards the expenses which would be incurred in publishing[50] a combined guide and catalogue. He also listed a number[60] of practical hints for the protection of our interests, and[70] a copy of these will be circulated to all members.[80] Subject to your approval, we shall accept the suggested grant,[90] as we consider it is the duty of this society[100] gladly to take all steps possible towards our stated goal.[110] The conditions attached to the actual making of the grant[120] are not unusual, and I trust that you will vote[130] in favour of its being accepted. (136)

" C." Vocabulary for Outline Drill

grid	conducts	execute	tightened	beautiful
pits	cant	Bude	straightened	pitiful
cheats	struggled	Bedford	quite	protect
referred	draft	endowed	quiet	predict
reserved	gifts	kid	gentleman	identical
mortal	extends	codes	agent	imperturbable
currently	grand	boots	support	expenditure
apparently	hunting	critic	separate	prejudice-d-ial-ly
arranged	merchants	greetings	secret	
concludes	kindred	doted	sacred	

Dictation Practice

(73) Ladies and Gentlemen, I am glad to have the honour[10] of taking the chair to-day and of extending to all[20] of you, on behalf of the Board, a most hearty[30] welcome. The report and accounts setting out the trading results[40] for last year were dispatched to you several days ago,[50] and it will be apparent to you all that, while[60] we have struggled to protect our business, we have been[70] hard hit in many directions and have encountered many obstacles.[80] Nor are things likely to be better during the current[90] year. Indeed, I cannot predict the likely course of our[100] trading during the current year. I can merely say that[110] we remain imperturbable in the face of difficulty, knowing that[120] such an old-established firm of merchant dealers cannot easily[130] be knocked out of the market. Actually, we have not[140] suffered to quite the same extent as certain kindred businesses[150] owing to the conservative basis on which we have conducted[160] our affairs in the past. We have always made it[170] a practice that our resources should be conserved as far[180] as was possible, and the sums reserved in good years[190] will stand us in excellent stead in the present difficult[200] years. Last year I referred to the growing grip upon[210] us of outside control, and this grip has been greatly[220] tightened in recent weeks. While I do not wish to[230] appear to be a critic of the Government, it has[240] not escaped my notice that a certain prejudice seems occasionally[250] to operate against our direct interests. A constant watch has[260] to be kept by the Board to make sure that[270] we are not cheated of our legitimate rights, and we[280] are just now busy upon the drafting of a memorandum[290] which sets out clearly the requirements of this and allied[300] businesses. A meeting has been arranged which will take place[310] shortly, and while it is too early yet to conclude[320] that some agreement will be reached I can say that[330] I am putting aside all personal doubts and that I[340] am hopeful that a satisfactory line of conduct may be[350] arranged for both sides.   (354)

(74) (a) The inhabitants of this country are fortunate in living in[10] an exceptionally temperate climate, and the degree of heat experienced[20] habitually in desert lands is never approached here. In those[30] hot lands no clouds protect the earth from the fierce[40]

and blinding heat of the sun; no plants and vegetable[50] matter protect the ground. The earth becomes hot beyond anything[60] which can be imagined here; but the creatures of the[70] desert can adapt themselves and tolerate these high temperatures. They[80] can remain seated upon rocks which could not be touched by[90] hand. Hot periods in this country are infrequent but should[100] you be easily disturbed by the heat of a midsummer[110] day there are four rules which should be complied with.[120] In the first place, violent exercise should not be indulged[130] in; secondly, the skin should be kept perfectly conditioned so[140] that the pores can do their work without hindrance; tight[150] clothing should be avoided; and the diet should be adjusted[160] to ensure that heat-producing foods are not taken in[170] abundant quantities.   (172)

(*b*) saturating exhilarated adroit allotted adjourned deplete dissect interrupt latitude Egypt wielded petulance indisputable contestant interrogate intestate nitrate exasperate precipitated

PART TWO: Halving of Curved Strokes

" A." Vocabulary for Outline Drill

feet	relate	until	boards	that
not	demand	amount	world	without
thought	dearest	find	lead	hand
meet	flight	mind	sold	handle
east	comfort	needs	ready	under
arts	issued	modern	followed	understand
heart	limit	sound	married	third
late	little	made	effects	thirds
night	recently	thousand	minutes	short
methods	results	old	longed	shortly
built	sometimes	fields	meaty	immediate
left	systems	hard	badness	immediately

Dictation Practice

(75) Dear Mr. East, I have now been able to give[10] careful thought to the methods recently suggested by you for[20] meeting the increased demands made upon us of late weeks.[30] Until the present time, we have not for the most[40] part experienced any difficulty in making our present methods meet[50] all our needs, even though additional goods have had to[60] be handled without loss of time. Recently the Board have[70] found it hard work to meet modern needs under the[80] system built up in the past. The Board are therefore[90] ready to make an immediate change in their system of[100] handling goods and they are ready to consider the details[110] of your suggested system, which appeared to them to be[120] a sound one. At present we market more than a[130] thousand different lines of goods but this number is shortly[140] to be cut by more than a third. We have[150] already issued instructions for an immediate limit to be placed[160] upon the production of our dearest lines, following the lead[170] of

certain other undertakings in this particular field. Demand from[180] all parts of the world has naturally fallen off of[190] late but this has been more than off-set by[200] the greatly increased demand for the home market. We should[210] like to have a heart-to-heart talk with you[220] about the whole position. Yours truly,   (226)

" B." Vocabulary for Outline Drill

entire	admit	unite	afford	indicate
entirely	admitting	metal	fold	medical
fit	arrived	ant	tired	load
fat	effort	net	middle	lady
salt	fruit	nut	mailed	jellied
felt	lift	remained	sand	locate
shut	pleasant	feud	secured	miniature
cent	pleasantly	unit	shared	locked
evident	automatic	fund	standard	muddy
evidence	fertile	around	admired	needy
fighting	permit	concerned	lingered	flooding
sheet	generate	argument	enquired	attitude
knot	military	fortunate	repaired	tightness
estimate	senate	equipment	ordinary	individual-ly
absolute	sentiment	bird	revealed	
absolutely	shout	card	combed	

Dictation Practice

(76) Messrs. Read, Bird & Sons, 15 Lady Road, Oldham. Gentlemen,[10] Permit us to inform you that we have mailed to[20] you to-day by separate post estimates for work in accordance[30] with the particulars which you had the courtesy to submit[40] to us.

The motto of this undertaking is: "Never let[50] the grass grow under your feet" and all our employees[60] unite in their attempts to reach a high standard in[70] all work carried out by them. This pleasant unity of[80] effort is revealed in the results of the work, whether[90] we are undertaking an ordinary little job for the small[100] man or are supplying large quantities of equipment for a[110] world-famous combine. In these days no individual can afford[120] to risk delay or disappointment in the middle of a[130] contract. We are fortunately in a position to indicate that[140] once we have embarked on a contract all units concerned[150] go forward without argument towards the desired end, and because[160] of this attitude work goes through pleasantly and absolutely to[170] time. This is our guarantee to you should you decide[180] to put the work in our hands. Yours faithfully,   (189)

(77) The girl walked with light steps along the hot pavement.[10] Here and there knots of young men were standing around[20] gossiping idly in the middle of the little street, and[30] they would turn to watch her. Almost unconsciously they admired[40] the lift of her neat head, the tilt of her[50] soft chin, the thoughtless grace of her entire bearing. Her[60] vivid clothes, too, attracted notice; but if she knew that[70] she was admired or criticized as she made her way[80]

along the winding street, the knowledge was not revealed by[90] so much as a glance to the left or to[100] the right. For the girl the street remained empty of[110] other living creatures. The brilliant mid-day sun poured down upon[120] her uncovered head, and picked out the golden lights which[130] tried to hide in her chestnut curls. The tan which[140] gleamed through her open sandals indicated a nature which loved[150] the light of the sun and feared no ill effects.[160] The street along which she thus made her way was[170] quaint and old-fashioned. The low buildings leaned this way[180] and that, as if they were moved like men and[190] women by different moods. Here two roofs almost touched, there[200] an austere mood seemed to cause two walls to slant[210] away from each other. Apart from the young men, who[220] had white shady hats pulled down over their eyes, no[230] one else was about. The windows of the shops and[240] the houses were covered by green blinds which shut out[250] the fierce light and heat of the sun, and no[260] glimpse of the life which went on behind the windows[270] was revealed to the passer-by.   (275)

" C." Vocabulary for Outline Drill

shouting	renowned	medal	flamboyant	unavoidable
depreciate	islands	bombed	imbued	inevitable
approximately	refined	succumbed	evoked	endless
giant	ancient	acclaimed	mapped	needless
consistent	metric	scaled	select	learned
fertility	desultory	quailed	pallid	learn'ed
metallic	precedent	commend	corrode	intelligence
threats	Antwerp	defend	thronged	intelligent-ly
fountains	prevents	cured	tinkered	independent-ly-ce
velvet	quantities	madam	fingered	indispensable-ly
pilot	rudiments	indication	aptness	amalgamate
warned	Sheffield	ordinarily	unhesitatingly	amalgamated

Dictation Practice

(78) Mr. FitzGerald explained that while he felt honoured to be[10] in the chair he regretted that Mr. Middleton had telephoned[20] to say that he was compelled to be absent. All[30] those present would, however, appreciate that high executives like Mr.[40] Middleton were very rushed at the moment. It had been[50] Mr. Middleton's intention to speak on the subject of the[60] Board's stewardship during recent months. Mr. FitzGerald continued: "If it[70] is your wish I will say a few words regarding[80] the work wh'ch we have carried out and the profits[90] which have been earned. A necessary secrecy in the matter[100] of output prevents me from giving you an unqualified statement[110] of our position but the general course of our business[120] can be roughly mapped out for you. It is needless[130] for me to comment on the fact that this has[140] been no ordinary year for us. All precedents have inevitably[150] had 'to go by the board.' Anyone of independent mind[160] and with intelligence must realize that the recent steps taken[170] to amalgamate this undertaking with other

similar undertakings were unavoidable[180] in the special circumstances. I can unhesitatingly state that one[190] of the worst blows from which we have suffered is[200] the loss of our business in Antwerp. For some time[210] past business there had been carried out in a somewhat[220] desultory fashion but good profits had been earned right up[230] to the last moment. Unfortunately in September last a serious[240] fire occurred and the property was almost completely destroyed. The[250] eastern section of the factory was gutted, and the equipment[260] lost. Fortunately, the premises and plant were fully insured, but[270] the fact remains that there must inevitably be a heavy[280] loss consequent upon the cessation of production. The cause of[290] the fire is not yet known, but earnest efforts are[300] being made to ascertain the reason for the outbreak.   (309)

(79) (*a*) Sometimes we grow tired of drinking from the fountain from[10] which a steady flow of modern fiction is poured out[20] for us; sometimes we grow bored with the endless tales[30] of crime and passion, of people with strange standards and[40] warped minds; sometimes too our minds are not prepared to[50] entertain long and involved arguments on the causes which have[60] brought about the present distressed state of the world. We[70] want to shut out the ordinary hurrying life which we[80] find about us, we wish to escape into something pleasant[90] and remote. Then is the time to turn from the[100] modern writers to our favourite writers of the past. Those[110] of us who have loved the writings of Richard Jefferies[120] find it impossible to open his books without falling once[130] more a victim to his undoubted charm. As we read,[140] a pleasantly fertile and aromatic countryside passes before our eyes.[150] The 'pageant of summer' fascinates us as we watch it[160] floating gently past our enchanted gaze. Is there any other[170] writer who carries so absolute and certain a power to[180] make us see with his eyes, to think with his[190] mind, to rejoice with his heart, as the beauty of[200] the unspoiled fields and meadows unfolds before us, and their[210] mysteries are revealed?   (213)

(*b*) maimed annulled gambit dilute symmetry insinuate impaired emanate embodiment imperilled harangued assaults suffocate vehement censured deciphered poignant quarrelled transient

SECTION NINE: DOUBLING

" A." Vocabulary for Outline Drill

after	orders	December	leader	therefore
afternoon	nature	painters	better	rather, writer
father	ordering	longer	brother	writers
matter	another	planter	wintry	interest
mother	lighter	September	country	interested
further	materials	kinder	mattered	disinterested
motoring	winter	picture	ordered	
future	neither	frequenter	motored	
motors	distributor	older	pictured	

Dictation Practice

(80) My brother and I naturally took it as a matter[10] of course that we went motoring on the long afternoons[20] of summer. My father and mother would often tell us[30] that they were not interested in motoring, that older people[40] could not understand the interest of young people in such[50] things. But it somehow happened that whenever the motor-car[60] appeared at the door they were dressed and ready to[70] be taken for another drive into the country. They clearly[80] loved these drives, but throughout the afternoon they would present[90] us with a most unpleasing picture of the future of[100] the country. The future countryside they pictured would be one[110] with little plant or animal life, but with great wide[120] motoring roads along which would pass at great rates thousands[130] and thousands of long, low motor-cars, the people inside[140] them seeing little and caring nothing for the natural and[150] wonderful loveliness of the old countryside. Even in winter father[160] and mother could be found sitting in the back of[170] the car, looking with interested eyes upon the white and[180] wintry world through which we motored. Neither father nor mother[190] could drive, and we often told them that if father[200] were sitting in the driving position he would paint a[210] quite different picture of the future of motor-cars. (219)

" B." Vocabulary for Outline Drill

feature	centre	fender	Walter	powdered
latter	central	remainder	tender	powdery
feather	tutor	scatter	milder	wondered
Easter	inspectors	wonder	contributor	blundered
contractor	blunder	wander	murder	altered
splendour	alter	splinter	chamber	scattered
chapter	importer	structure	jumper	louder
powder	enters	neuter	hunger	ladders
operator	litter	render	lingers	entered
porter	exporter	builders	daughter	hungered
reporter	voters	disorder	factor	

Dictation Practice

(81) Among the lighter fiction published in December is another story[10] by Walter Porter called *Murder Wanders In.* The structure

of[20] the story is built of the materials which are a[30] feature of most detective stories The author scatters throughout his[40] chapters a wonderful mixture of characters. We first encounter the[50] central figures in all the splendour of their wealthy homes,[60] and from them we pass to a bewildering group of[70] importers and exporters, of bullying inspectors and heartless reporters. There[80] is the harmless old tutor and the beautiful daughter, the[90] fair telephone operator and the mysterious manager of the powder[100] factory. There is the usual litter of ladders and tenders[110] and secret chambers. But when, in the last chapter, we[120] hunger for some solution, for some order to come out[130] of all this amazing disorder, the criminal obligingly makes a[140] stupid blunder, and Inspector Peters emerges from the welter triumphant[150] once more—just as we knew that he would from[160] the first word of the first chapter. It is perhaps[170] not to be wondered at that we turn with some[180] relief from *Murder Wanders In* to the new edition of[190] the fairy tales of Hans Andersen, which is the outstanding[200] feature of the list of children's books. This is a[210] superb edition with the most delightful coloured pictures to illustrate[220] the stories. Miss Saunders is to be congratulated upon the[230] delicacy of her work. As for the fairy tales themselves,[240] they retain all their old wonder and enchantment. There is[250] the Tinder-Box and the dog with the eyes as[260] big as teacups. Here is the Marsh King's Daughter, and[270] there are the watchful storks. The charm of other fairy[280] tales may grow dim, but for some reason or other[290] the tales of Hans Andersen are always bright.   (298)

(82) Messrs. Drifter & Sons, Contractors, 14 Andrew Square, Sunderland. Dear[10] Sirs, Thank you for your letter of the 14th September.[20] We note that you are moving your Headquarters to a[30] more central position, and we agree with you that this[40] should not in any way alter our present relations with[50] you. We regret to note, however, that you are proposing[60] to alter your charges when the remainder of the period[70] of our contract has been served. You may remember that[80] we entered into this contract with you in spite of[90] the fact that another firm of contractors were offering lower[100] rates. At the beginning of September we received a letter[110] from the latter stating that they would not be altering[120] their charges at least until the end of December. In[130] other words, they find it unnecessary at present to alter[140] their comparatively low rates while your firm, for some reason[150] or other, apparently find it necessary to increase their already[160] high charges. In these circumstances we cannot see our way[170] to renew our contract with you when the remainder of[180] the present term has run out. Yours truly, Porters &[190] Chambers.   (191)

" C." **Vocabulary for Outline Drill**

meander	saunter	diameter	temper	Luther
fetters	Sutherland	calendar	plumper	leather
sisters	Cinderella	sectors	rancour	neutral
oyster	leaseholder	squander	feathery	natural
charter	Canterbury	speculator	boundary	further
borders	slaughter	refrigerator	inventory	farther
structural	wilderness	indicator	thundered	captor
thither	elevators	rafters	sauntered	capture
inventor	Anderson	reminder	pampered	raptor
dictator	householder	shareholder	rendered	rapture
educator	thermometer	pamper	auditor	arbitrator
shatter	Sunderland	timber	juncture	entertainment

Dictation Practice

(83) At the 25th annual general meeting of the Henderson[10] Refrigerator Company, Mr. Anderson, Managing Director, said: The calendar shows[20] it to be only a matter of months since last[30] we met here but if measured by events rather than[40] by the calendar it would seem to be a matter[50] of years. Certain countries have decided upon a régime of[60] competition which has rendered, and will continue to render, it[70] impossible for peace-loving countries to saunter along in their[80] old ways. I need not squander time, however, by saying[90] anything further on these lines, as we know only too[100] well the competitive temper of the times. An immediate effect[110] of the competition has been to shatter our expressed hopes[120] of increasing the sales of our refrigerators during the current[130] year by 50 per cent. When we last met I[140] stated that we looked forward to the time when every[150] householder of average income would own a Henderson Refrigerator, and[160] that we were looking forward to an early capture of[170] several markets overseas. While some of these overseas countries remain[180] friendly, we unfortunately find ourselves farther from the capture of[190] the markets than formerly. Indeed, we are seriously cutting down[200] the manufacture of refrigerators and are turning our attention to[210] the manufacture of articles of a more general nature. There[220] has been a drop in our sale of refrigerators to[230] restaurants, as with the increasing popularity of television the restaurants[240] in their turn have experienced a falling off of customers.[250] Shareholders will be interested to learn that there is a[260] brisk demand for our Luther Thermometers, the sales of these[270] thermometers having almost doubled. Those of our products which depend[280] upon an ample supply of timber are being greatly restricted[290] and we are hampered in all directions by the difficulty[300] of obtaining the necessary raw materials. Manufacturers of synthetic materials,[310] however, state that in their opinion it is merely a[320] matter of time before satisfactory substitutes are provided. Shareholders may[330] like a reminder that there will be an interval of[340] one hour after this meeting, when another meeting is to[350] take place. (352)

(84) (*a*) Inventors are always at work, and these inventors and their[10] collaborators find new terms for their inventions. Our vocabularies are[20] therefore always growing, and the present generation can talk easily[30] of distributors and carburettors, of diesel-dumpers and micrometers, of[40] precision grinders and steam-generators, of reflectors and hydrometers.   (49)

(*b*) concentric riveters insulator cylindrical sombre commentator intercepted rejoinder caterpillar intermittent exhibitor intersected navigator perambulator interrogatory

SECTION TEN: STROKES eL, W-L, WH-L, LeR, AND iSH

"A." Vocabulary for Outline Drill

coal	sell	rule	wells	fishing
family	sold	until	willing	fisher
follow	relation	additional	while	electric
milk	look	senseless	whilst	electricity
pull	love	lessens	field	electrical
detail	liking	rulers	she	publisher
hold	long	fuller	shipment	English
July	along	controller	machine	insurance
later	full	well	official	
health	only	will	shilling	

Dictation Practice

(85) The official handbook is called "Your Family and the Coal[10] Question." The handbook is sold at one shilling a copy,[20] and the publisher says that it has been written by[30] Mr. Fisher, who is the Coal Controller for this city.[40] Great care has been taken to show the public the[50] real relation between coal and electricity, and the best uses[60] which can be made of both. Many pictures of valuable[70] electrical machines are given, along with long accounts of the[80] industrial fields in which they are most useful. While the[90] immediate purposes of the book are well served, however, the[100] writer has gone to the additional trouble of making sure[110] that the book will please those who love good writing.[120] As a rule, these official handbooks are poorly written and[130] show a cold official mind working along cold official lines;[140] but while no doubt Mr. Fisher is the usual English[150] official in many respects he at least understands how senseless[160] it is to publish handbooks which are not easily understood[170] by the man in the street. Another little handbook is[180] to be published shortly giving details of the National Health[190] Insurance Act. The fact that many people do not understand[200] this Act greatly lessens its value, and it is hoped[210] that the book will give the people a fuller understanding[220] of the field covered by the insurance. (227)

"B." Vocabulary for Outline Drill

loyal	valley	lose	soil	gentle
deal	envelopes	loudly	level	nail
else	fellow	delay	island	scale
slopes	hall	sleep	lack	skill
ill	hill	boiling	laid	actually
absolute	collar	bulb	launch	election
allies	cool	mental	lion	exactly
solid	lake	involve	loan	files
bells	laugh	mail, male	local	filling
bills	legs	female	load	listen
dealers	length	soldier	lie	lessons
delight	lips	lay	retailer	muscles

previously	availed	shoes	push	shell
false	walls	shape	shame	brush
unless	wheels	share	shock	pressure
fails	insure	sheet	smash	shelf
alone	insured	sheep	shirt	Lord
awful	wash	cash	foolish	efficiency-t-ly
scholar	rush	shop	social	
valour	shade	shore	sugar	
avail	shake	polish	shoulder	

Dictation Practice

(86) Experts on psychology tell us that the colour scheme of[10] our homes will affect our whole lives. It will affect[20] our sleep and also our outlook during hours of daylight[30] and hours of artificial light. We all appreciate the fact[40] that colour may be used to alter the apparent shape[50] of a room, and to add to or lessen the[60] apparent length of walls. Colour may be used to make[70] rooms look smaller or more spacious, to suggest coolness or[80] a welcome warmth. Skill in the selection and blending of[90] colours is actually rarely found among untrained people, for it[100] involves a fuller knowledge of colour values than most of[110] us possess naturally, and the advice of a specialist is[120] invaluable. Some people are foolish enough and childish enough to[130] follow social fashions in this matter, with results that are[140] generally false and sometimes awful. It is foolish in the[150] extreme to rush to give our walls a wash of[160] bright red distemper and our ceilings a wash of black[170] distemper merely because we have just listened to our friends[180] speaking loudly in praise of such a colour scheme in[190] the lounge of Lord Charles, the local celebrity. It is[200] well not to launch out upon a violently new colour[210] scheme unless it has been well considered previously. The palatial[220] house demands different treatment from the small bungalow, the town[230] villa from the country cottage. It is well worth while[240] to spend a little of our leisure on the study[250] of colour, as efficiency in this respect may influence our[260] health and the shape of our lives. We are informed[270] that some colours, such as green, should be used in[280] large quantities only in rooms which have plenty of sunlight[290] as they absorb light; but almost any colour can be[300] successfully utilized in small amounts to give good relative colour[310] accents. A good general rule is that a cool colour[320] scheme needs a few warm shades to give balance, while[330] a warm scheme needs neutral shades to prevent it from[340] being garish. Further, the actual materials influence the selection of[350] colours, and certain shades while beautiful on a glossy surface[360] are merely dull on a matt surface. Unless a whole[370] room is to be newly furnished, existing carpets and furnishing[380] fabrics must be considered. The illusion of sunshine can be[390] obtained by painting the walls a deep yellow near the[400] floor and gradually lessening the depth of yellow until it[410] is quite pale towards the ceiling.   (416)

" C." Vocabulary for Outline Drill

allowance	indulge	yells	British	efficient-ly-cy
colleagues	realization	skulls	brushing	deficient-ly-cy
fittingly	relativity	secular	appreciation	sufficient-ly-cy
excelling	entail	dweller	shampoo	proficient-ly-cy
idealize	stylish	wild	splasher	influential-ly
evolving	dwelling	wool	martial	England
impels	licences	Welsh	laboured	legislative
smiles	obsolescence	whales	elaborate	legislature
boiling	aluminium	shears	convulsion	questionable-y
locker	allocation	shack	evolution	unquestionable-y
callous	facile	shone	valuable	
casual	nails	shirts	available	
Leslie	vessels	astonish	fatal	
lungs	realm	Polish	futile	

Dictation Practice

(87) From the laboratories of the world come artificial products which[10] until recently could be obtained only in their natural forms.[20] Napoleon started an industry for the extraction of sugar from[30] beet, and in our laboratories to-day cellulose can be split[40] up into sugar. Rayon is an artificial silk which is[50] cheaper to produce than real silk. As rayon is now[60] available on a sufficiently wide scale to meet most requirements,[70] the demand for real silk has unquestionably fallen. Artificial wool[80] is an efficient substitute for real wool, and Italians manufacture[90] large quantities of artificial wool from a material which they[100] obtain from tinned milk. This artificial wool washes better than[110] the real article. One of the latest substances to be[120] put on the market is nylon, and nylon unquestionably has[130] a wonderful future. Nylon can be made into fibres which[140] are finer, stronger, and more elastic than the fibres of[150] real silk, and cloth made from it is actually more[160] proficient in many ways than real silk. Nylon can be[170] made into many things, including bristles for toothbrushes and nailbrushes.[180] It is already quite common to see advertisements of brushes[190] with bristles made from nylon. Nylon is manufactured chiefly from[200] coal-tar products, such as carbolic acid, and therefore can[210] be made wherever coal is available. Bakelite is a well-[220]known plastic which is largely used for ash-trays, electric[230] fittings, etc., but it is immensely valuable in many directions.[240] It can be used for bearings and cogwheels in machinery,[250] but the latest triumph is the aeroplane which is now[260] undergoing proficiency trials in America. The bakelite fuselage of the[270] machine is moulded in one piece by a huge mould[280] which, worked by nine men, can turn out ten fuselages[290] per day.   (292)

(88) (a) The work of Mr. J. B. Priestley is very popular[10] both in England and elsewhere, for his writing appeals to[20] a wide audience. In the world of the theatre his[30] skill has won for him the appreciation of thousands of[40] experienced theatre-goers; in the realm of

essay-writing he[50] has shone for many years; and in the realm of[60] popular fiction his admirers must surely be numbered in millions.[70] When Mr. Priestley writes a serious book it is very[80] serious indeed, and it is also exceedingly good literature. His[90] popular novels are, however, gigantic fairy tales. Fairy tales, however,[100] carry morals and so do Mr. Priestley's novels, but the[110] pill is offered to us in the most palatable form.[120] He may write a likeable piece of fooling but tucked[130] away among the laughs is a criticism of our way[140] of living. The element of slapstick which steals into his[150] lighter work may not be appreciated by those who scorn[160] to relish a little nonsense, but those of us who[170] love Priestley's work appreciate the slapstick along with the rest.   (180)

(*b*) lacerate lackadaisical aniline unlicensed lavishly threshold fallacious Shanghai veracious facetious hallucination electrolysis superstitious illiterate woollen electron lucre laminate

SECTION ELEVEN: STROKES aR, Ray, AND ReR

"A." Vocabulary for Outline Drill

rates	reason	answers	warmth	yard
rich	turn	disappear	colours	word
wrong	where	quarters	colouring	regular
relation	experience	air	clearer	irregular
authority	history	army	poorer	responsible-ity
charges	modern	car	cleared	irresponsible-ity
marriage	morning	fear	board	satisfactory
carry	expert	art	are	respect-ed
memory	operate	hear	our, hour	respective
earth	support	iron	your	respectively
railway	certainly	orderly	year	

Dictation Practice

(89) No doubt you have taken the opportunity to read the[10] report of our year's work, and I do not think[20] that it is necessary for me to run through the[30] report here. On the whole, I think we are right[40] in regarding the report as satisfactory in most respects but[50] it would be wrong to expect our operations to show[60] equally good results during the present year. Only those of[70] us who are in authority and who have the responsibility[80] for carrying on the work of your company can fully[90] understand the power of the forces which are now operating[100] against our success. Our history during the last twenty years[110] has been happier than that of many organizations with whom[120] we are in direct competition, and we trust that our[130] satisfactory experiences during good years will stand us in good[140] part in these serious modern times. Those of you with[150] memories of our difficulties during the war of 25[160] years ago will understand partly what we are up against,[170] particularly in the matter of our overseas trade. The Board[180] no doubt have a clearer picture of events in all[190] quarters than is possible for most of you present to-day,[200] and we trust therefore with all our hearts that you[210] will continue to give us your support even though future[220] results may appear to be poorer.   (226)

" B." Vocabulary for Outline Drill

receipts	riches	born	pure	artillery
rocks	riding	corn	pursue	remaining
rowing	rise	circle	reply	remittance
rapid	rolls	prepare	replied	removal
rapidity	roof	resource	birth	ears
raising	roses	terrible	berry	admire
rank	rub	various	rice	affairs
range	raining	vary	ring	enforce
realize	arch	theory	rhythm	cork
recognize	narrow	library	etcetera	forks
recognition	foreign	trousers	factory	tear
refer	fourth	territory	forthwith	inspire
refuse	American	glory	closer	pairs
requests	article	merchandise	assure	dollars

errors	dare	hair	persevere	admirer
fair	declare	per	bear	wearer
firm	floor	securing	bore	admired
fur	arrive	wear	burst	declared

Dictation Practice

(90) *From the Work Room and Services and Repair Department*
Madam :[10] We know that you, as a wearer of good furs,[20] will recognize the real worth of keeping your furs in[30] a state of excellent repair. This firm, as you will[40] be aware, offers an expert service in this respect. To[50] our regret, however, we have now to inform you that[60] we can foresee many difficulties in the early future regarding[70] the execution of orders for remodelling, repairing, or restoring your[80] own furs. Further, the present trend of affairs makes it[90] clear that there will be a rise in the prices[100] of materials and accessories used in such work, and salaries[110] will also rise. May we recommend you therefore to try[120] to foresee your particular requirements in the matter of these[130] expert services, and let us execute the work for you[140] at the earliest possible moment? Should you wish to secure[150] new furs at reasonable prices, we suggest that you visit[160] our showrooms, where you will see our new models. These[170] models are bound to inspire your admiration in respect to[180] both style and price. Hoping to be favoured with early[190] instructions, We are, Yours faithfully,   (195)

(91) Robinson had been riding rapidly towards the red brick factory[10] which could be clearly seen in the distance, but now[20] he held the reins more loosely and looked around him.[30] He recognized and rejoiced in the richness of the surrounding[40] countryside. It had been raining heavily, and the rising hills[50] to the right now took on the colours of the[60] vivid rainbow which arched the sky. Raindrops quivering on leaves[70] and grasses reflected the same lovely colours, and Robinson had[80] a momentary vision of pure glory. But the glory passed,[90] the storm clouds gathered again, and he was aware that[100] the rain had soaked his trousers and that the factory[110] towards which he was riding was preparing to use all[120] its powerful and terrible resources for purposes which to him[130] were evil. What course of action to pursue was the[140] question which baffled him, and which startled him, because the[150] answer should have been easier than he found it. Once[160] he had been the centre of a circle of admiring[170] and worshipping men, and if he persevered in his refusal[180] to carry on with his work in the normal way[190] he would now earn the scorn and ill-wishes of[200] these same men who, with rough and ready thinking, declared[210] that they cared nothing for ultimate purposes but much for[220] the immediate returns which big contracts offered. Robinson jerked on[230] the reins, and the horse trotted on.   (237)

"G." Vocabulary for Outline Drill

restive	theorize	armaments	reserves	arbitration
raucous	erudition	artful	resources	arbitrary
wrathful	artisan	Rumania	pure	familiarize
recourse	artesian	inspiration	poor	executor
rhythmic	orgy	rheumatism	purpose	recoverable
respite	originate	Cork	propose	reform-ed
territorial	adherence	Arthur	persecute	perform-ed
parsnips	disburse	urgent	prosecute	performance
careers	Edinburgh	porter	birth	architect-ure-al
Barnes	carrots	shirts	burial	emergency
Derby	grosser	insurer	purchaser	republic
pursuance	cruiser	explorer	predecessor	republican

Dictation Practice

(92) The market report states that security markets continue to preserve[10] a tone of calmness. Prices in certain directions shaded off,[20] reflecting the poorer trading conditions, but while the market was[30] restive at times the result was to restrict business rather[40] than to bring about an orgy of selling. Rubber is[50] being quoted at fourteen pence per pound. Among iron ores[60] Westerns reacted to 31⅛. Moderate losses were reported[70] in some respects. Imperial Tobaccos are quoted at[80] 87s. 6d., Woolworths at 48s. 6d.,[90] and Marks and Spencers at 34s. Barrow and[100] Staines have lowered to 20s. 9d. while Turners[110] at 56s. show a narrow fall. Most rayons[120] are steady and there is relative steadiness in the steel[130] section, purchasers buying Allied Iron at 11s. Gold shares[140] are scarcely maintaining their price. Rolls Royce are falling slightly,[150] and Far Eastern Bonds show improvement. The declaration of a[160] dividend of 5 per cent per annum by the Republican[170] Rail Corporation has stimulated interest in the preference shares.   (179)

(93) (a) Some people turn their minds into a store-house of[10] memories. The glories of the past inspire in them a[20] worship which nothing in the present can seriously disturb. But[30] it is an arbitrary rule of life that memories of[40] the past form a poor substitute for the realities of[50] the present; and those with a more realistic outlook will[60] declare that one happy hour to-day is worth six happy[70] hours in years gone by. But there are times when[80] it is worth while to retain in our minds a[90] memory of the past, and all of us have experienced[100] delightful moments which we can recall when current events reveal[110] little that is beautiful. I recently arrived at the house[120] of my Aunt Ruth to find her sitting on the[130] floor, turning the pages of an album with reverent fingers.[140] "Come here, Irene," she said, "and look at this." I[150] recognized a picture of Madame Anna Pavlova, foremost ballerina and[160] dancer of our era. With Aunt Ruth I was back[170] through the years. We had waited for four hours in[180] the Gallery queue outside the Covent Garden Opera House, sharing[190] a narrow-seated stool. But

at last the doors opened,[200] and we began the mad haphazard rush upstairs to the[210] Gallery. Flight after flight of stairs were necessarily taken at[220] a run so that others could not race past and[230] secure the better seats for which we had so patiently[240] waited. But a wait of four hours was unworthy of[250] mention if at the end of it we were privileged[260] to see a performance by Anna Pavlova, inspired dancer, enchanted[270] artiste. To the immature she is but an empty name[280] but those who can recapture the spell of her dancing[290] in all its glorious beauty have a memory worth preserving[300] throughout life.   (302)

(*b*) rapacity resuscitate forcible reticence irreplaceable reverberated extortionate reciprocity navicerts recalcitrant irruption aggressor aberration rigorously rescind menagerie rationalize embarrassing rudimentary.

SECTION TWELVE: THE ASPIRATE;
" OMISSIONS " IN PHRASES

" A." Vocabulary for Outline Drill

happy	house	higher	heart	girlhood
happiest	hundred	highly	help	perhaps
head	behind	highest	her	household
heavy	boyhood	home	held	unhealthy
half	heat	whom	horse	
happen	height	hard	whole	
history	he	here	wholesome	
historical	high	herewith	health	

Dictation Practice

(94) Some of the happiest days of his boyhood had been[10] spent on horseback. He had first learned to sit well[20] on a horse when he was still in his childhood,[30] for his father had believed deeply in the natural friendship[40] which appears to exist between man and horse, and had[50] thought it a good wholesome and healthy way of spending[60] the morning hours. But boyhood days had been left far[70] behind him, and the history of the household in the[80] "years between" had been the history of hard times. Perhaps[90] the hardest thing that had happened to him since he[100] came of age had been the necessary selling up of[110] the old home, the parting with the horses, the breaking[120] up of the grounds, with all their long historical background.[130] Watching his own youngster playing happily outside, he remembered the[140] day when he had walked through the house for the[150] last time with his father. Their heads had been held[160] down and their step had been heavy. The impossible had[170] happened, and he and his father had left the large[180] white house. Even the house existed no longer, for the[190] buyer had pulled it down and in its place there[200] was now a modern home. But, he told himself, he[210] must always keep in mind that if his boy had[220] no horses and no large house he at least had[230] a happy and healthy childhood. (235)

" B." Vocabulary for Outline Drill

hang	hesitation	behaviour	hollow	vehicle
heaven	hive	hairs	horn	inhospitable
hurry	unhurried	halls	hoarse	inherit
hide	behave	hills	human	inhabit
husband	hat	Hampstead	hump	
hero	hot	hurt	unhurt	
hence	hook	harbour	uphill	
hunts	hay	harmony	mishear	

Dictation Practice

(95) Henry Hobbs, the owner of the horse-drawn vehicle, states[10] that he was proceeding in an unhurried manner uphill towards[20]

the main Hammersmith road. He was leading his horse, walking[30] along beside the horse's head. He was close to the[40] hedge, and as it was a hot afternoon he had[50] stopped for a few moments just before he reached the[60] bridge with the hump back. He removed his hat and[70] watched the behaviour of a group of young men who[80] were lightheartedly turning the hay in the fields at the[90] foot of the hills. He had gone only a few[100] more yards when he heard a hoarse cry behind him :[110] "Look out, mister!" A huge lorry was tearing down the[120] bridge towards him at a terrific speed. Without hesitating a[130] second Hobbs turned the head of his horse into the[140] hedge, and the lorry crashed into the side of his[150] cart and turned over on its side. To his relief[160] and surprise both the driver and his mate crawled unhurt[170] from the general wreckage, but as is human in such[180] cases there was a difference of opinion as to the[190] cause of the accident and each man put more or[200] less the whole of the blame upon the other. The[210] haymakers who hurried to the scene cannot give a completely[220] coherent story of the affair but on the whole they[230] seem to corroborate the evidence of Hobbs, whose horse was[240] frightened but not hurt in any way. The cart was,[250] of course, splintered. (253)

" C." Vocabulary for Outline Drill

honey	upheld	harmonize	mahogany	hearty
hitch	adhere	harness	apprehensive	hardy
hurricane	unheeding	humility	misapprehension	human
heaping	hoot	humbug	leaseholder	humane
hedges	hook	harvested	warmhearted	henceforward
horoscope	Higgins	Hamilton	brotherhood	howsoever
hammering	Hackney	hammock	inheritance	
hostel	hoax	hilarity	inhalation	
hitherto	hired	incoherence	inhumanity	

Dictation Practice

(96) Messrs. Harry Heywood & Heath, Hatters, Hogs Road, High Market.[10] Dear Sirs, With regard to the visit paid to us[20] last week by your traveller, Mr. Harold Hicks, we have[30] examined very carefully the list of prices which he left[40] with us and have concluded that we were under a[50] misapprehension when we complained to you last month about the[60] undue rise in your prices. There must have been some[70] error in our figures and we regret our hasty action.[80] In the circumstances, we have pleasure in enclosing an order[90] for spring hats selected from the styles shown to us[100] by Mr. Hicks. We trust that it will be possible[110] for you to hasten delivery as demand is brisk. Yours[120] faithfully, (121)

(97) (a) Mr. Hugh Hodges, Member for High Hackney, said that he[10] regretted that such a lack of harmony should be displayed[20] in a matter which affected every inhabitant of these islands.[30] He

heartily believed that an inharmonious atmosphere was not the[40] vehicle for reasoned thinking. Some Members had shown a spirit[50] of hilarity quite out of place in the House at[60] the present time; other Members had been more or less[70] incoherent. He might be under a misapprehension but he thought[80] that the matter had not been given that humane consideration[90] which it undoubtedly deserved. (94)

(b) histrionic Himalayan homogeneous hypothetical harass hector heinous heterogeneous

SECTION THIRTEEN: CONSONANTS
Way, WHay, WeL, WHeL, KWay, AND GWay

" A." Vocabulary for Outline Drill

way	weather	warm	well	with
away	Wednesday	were	will	when
weight	went	wire	while	what
watch	wasted	work	awhile	would
window	wide	world	quick	beyond
between	wise	worth	require	whatever
railway	winter	quality	sweets	whenever
once	otherwise	frequently	sweeten	whensoever
western	weak	herewith	unsweetened	whatsoever
want	walk	white	we	whereinsoever
water	war	where	whether	

Dictation Practice

(98) The weather was of a quality not infrequently met with[10] in the west just before winter sets in. It was[20] warm, and the wide waters which reached almost to the[30] door of the little house were still. As we watched[40] from the windows we could see the women from the[50] farms working hard in the fields. Trains were not frequent[60] in this part of the world, but now and again[70] one would pass along the high railway. While we could[80] hardly hear the trains we could see them well enough.[90] One old woman always stopped her work to watch the[100] train as it went heavily on its way. But on[110] the whole there was little waste of time in the[120] fields that day, for the farm workers were "weather wise"[130] and they knew that one hour's work that week was[140] worth two hours a week or two later, for the[150] weather would soon break and winter would be upon them.[160] There was no question whatsoever but that the work must[170] be done quickly and done well. There were people in[180] the distant towns who, knowing so little of the sweetness[190] of the countryside, were yet waiting for the products of[200] that countryside to help them to carry on with their[210] different but equally important kind of work. (217)

" B." Vocabulary for Outline Drill

wash	win	worry	wool	queen
wind	wound	worse	wall	quietly
wine	wage	twelve	wheel	liquid
wood	won	twenty	wild	square
waves	wife	qualify	wheat	swing
wing	witness	somewhat	enquiry	persuading
wet	wax	needlework	enquire	
twist	worm	whip	quotation	
awake	wagon	whistle	quantity	

Dictation Practice

(99) Messrs. Watson & Webster, 81 Waterloo Street, Wakefield. Gentlemen,[10] In response to your enquiry, we are enclosing

herewith copy[20] of our latest price list, with special quotations for bulk[30] orders of our Queen Weave woollen wear. We have already[40] witnessed a widespread increase in the price of all woollen[50] goods, and you will be fully awake to the fact[60] that it is a wise policy to place orders for[70] large quantities now while prices are low and the market[80] is quiet. Owing to forward buying, we are well able[90] just now to supply woollen goods, white or coloured, in[100] winter weight or light weight quality, and we do not[110] think you will require persuading of the wisdom of early[120] purchase. Without any question whatsoever, there will be a wave[130] of buying as soon as winter approaches, with consequent increases[140] in price. Further, it will be very difficult in future[150] to maintain the high quality of wool used in these[160] garments. As you know, our woollen goods are famous for[170] washing well, and special tests have shown that after twenty[180] hard washes the goods are none the worse for wear.[190] We trust that you will see your way to place[200] an order within the next few days for large quantities[210] of our Queen Weave woollen goods of all weights. Yours[220] faithfully,   (221)

(100) While we human beings have no natural means of keeping[10] warm in winter time, we have won our battle with[20] the creatures of the wilds and can use their warm[30] coverings to supply warmth for our own bodies. When we[40] witness the approach of winter we begin to wear clothes[50] made from wool or from fur. Well-clad ourselves, we[60] look out upon the wintry world and wonder how the[70] wild animals manage to withstand the rigours of the winter[80] when we, wearing extra clothes, seem to wither up under[90] the attack of the icy winds. But animals have their[100] own ways of waging war against the cold. Some grow[110] thicker or longer coats of hair or wool. Among the[120] wild creatures in very cold countries there is a tendency[130] for the colour of the animal's coat to change to[140] white as the grip of winter tightens on the land,[150] and of course in very cold countries the coats of[160] some wild animals are white all the year round. If[170] we wonder what causes this change to the white winter[180] dress, scientists will explain that the white hairs are really[190] the new growth of hairs, although some of the old[200] summer coat changes to white also. It appears that there[210] are two principal advantages to the wearer of the white[220] winter coat. The first is that there is much less[230] loss of body warmth if the body is covered with[240] white hairs or white feathers, and the second is that[250] a white dress is not conspicuous among the snowy wastes.[260]

The life of the creatures of the wild is made[270] up of a ceaseless war waged against one another and[280] against the forces of nature. It is a war in[290] which the hardy survive, and these white winter coats help[300] their owners to win part of that war.   (308)

" C." Vocabulary for Outline Drill

widow	wandering	sandwich	wield	linguist
Ottawa	Winnipeg	misquote	Wolverhampton	sanguine
weeding	wares	disqualify	Wallis	swanking
unworthy	worst	whirl	wheels	swirling
Worcester	wearily	wharf	wheelwright	swerve
qualifying	ward	whisper	acquire	unswerving
wins, wince	warehouses	whack	requisition	wheresoever
wanton	weariness	whitewash	equip	whithersoever
waver	warning	welding	quarrelsome	woman
waned	subsequently	welter	squire	women
weapons	Shadwell	Wellington	squadron	

Dictation Practice

(101) The Chairman, in reply, said that while he did not[10] wish to weary his audience with further worrying details he[20] wished to make it clear that Mr. Squires had misquoted[30] him. He did not wish to quarrel with Mr. Squires[40] and he welcomed worthy criticism, but he felt that the[50] statements made were unworthy of a gentleman and in the[60] worst possible taste. He did not wish to whitewash those[70] who had proved unable to wield worthily the power which[80] they had acquired, and he believed that the weeding out[90] of undesirable members of the company had been necessary; but[100] this weeding had been done twelve months ago and any subsequent[110] discussions became somewhat wearisome. He would like to give those[120] present an unqualified assurance that the Board would not waver[130] in their watch and ward over the interests of the[140] company and that there had been no waning of their[150] belief that the company was in a wholesome and well-[160]secured position. At the same time he had to warn[170] members that they would be taking an unduly sanguine view[180] if they expected widespread improvements in the quantity or quality[190] of their services during the current twelve months. In spite[200] of the immense and increasing wealth of this country, they[210] had to contend with widespread forces, and no one could[220] deny that there was a world-wide depression in trade[230] and industry at the present time.   (236)

(102) (*a*) The gardener who sets to work with the most sanguine[10] heart and the most unswerving devotion to his art cannot[20] long remain unaware that weeds will grow twice as quickly[30] as his most treasured flowers, that wild flowers will grow[40] twenty times more profusely than his most well-watered plants.[50] His expensive seedlings will wither and die during a dry[60] spell, but the unwelcome intruder will flourish exceedingly. The swift[70] downpour of rain, which wantonly washes away most of the[80] little seeds so carefully planted the night before, will fail[90] to disturb the activities of the wild plants which seem[100] able to withstand the wildest shower and even to welcome[110] it with unqualified enthusiasm. In a charming essay on wild[120] nature, Oliver Wendell Holmes says that he

knows nothing sweeter[130] than the way in which nature will leak in through[140] the cracks of walls and floors. If we heap a[150] million tons of stone on a square mile or two[160] of earth, the tiny plants on the hillsides will watch[170] us, and will whisper to one another: "Wait awhile." The[180] whisper passes from one to another, the years roll by,[190] and the wild plants saunter in one by one until[200] at last they come in swarms. And if we wait[210] for long enough we find that they have taken complete[220] possession of what was once the pride of human labour. (230)

(*b*) assuage consequential Wordsworth Willoughby whetted warrantable wharves quadruple squalor Quixotic ubiquitous welkin dwindled squalid whey wreathe woebegone unwieldy languorous

SECTION FOURTEEN : ABBREVIATING DEVICES

PART ONE: Prefixes and Suffixes

" A." Vocabulary for Outline Drill

complete	reconsider	immaterial	friendly	backward
control	discomfort	teaching	unfriendly	forward
consider	uncommon	ordering	citizenship	onward
competition	uncomfortable	hearing	relationship	onwards
conditions	self-control	running	hardships	backyard
commitment	self-important	meetings	carefulness	shipyard
common	self-made	painting	hopefulness	govern-ed
company	self-willed	dying	usefulness	government
comforts	illimitable	buying	carelessness	instructions
connections	known	announcement	hopelessness	instructive
continue	unknown	announcements	uselessness	

Dictation Practice

(103) Upon hearing the announcement of some new discovery we often[10] look for further details, and find that the man responsible[20] for the discovery is someone unknown to the world until[30] that moment. We probably find—and this was particularly true[40] in the past—that he has been working in uncomfortable[50] conditions and among unfriendly people who considered that he was[60] a little out of his mind. He has had to[70] use much self-control, to think lightly of discomfort and hardship,[80] and to be completely under the influence of the work[90] which he considers will, when completed, take people another step[100] forward in their onward march. Often the man has had[110] few personal friendships, caring little for the company of other[120] men or women. If he has at times experienced a[130] feeling of hopelessness, of the uselessness of his labours, he[140] has had to turn his mind away from such thoughts[150] and to reconsider the deep usefulness and the great possibilities[160] of his work. These unknown men have worked in backyards[170] and in little rooms; but they have been self-willed and[180] strong of purpose, and their powers of work seemed illimitable.[190] The final product of their labours is clear, but we[200] know little of the self-control and complete disregard for personal[210] comfort which made that product possible. (216)

" B." Vocabulary for Outline Drill

command	consume	accomplish	illegal	dispatching
confer	convenience	introducing	irresistible	catching
concerning	complain	magnificent	immovable	plating
conclude	consist	transport	attaching	ploughing
conduct	constitute	self-contained	eating	posting
confidence	convince	self-possession	dancing	bearings
complex	unconvincing	self-conscious	wondering	pumping
contain	unconscious	instruct	requesting	achieving
construct	accompany	instruments	piping	pocketing

swimming	pavement	fondly	harmfulness	Edward
popularity	achievement	blindly	faithfulness	
majority	experimental-ly	urgently	sleeplessness	
inability	instrumental-ly	ladyship	faithlessness	
psychological-ly	tenderly	lordship	rewards	

Dictation Practice

(104) Dear Sir or Madam, Are you conscious of desiring to[10] achieve popularity with the majority of people around you and[20] yet conscious of your inability to win this popularity? Do[30] you seek for higher achievements in your work or in[40] your sport and recreations? Do you dream of achieving magnificent[50] accomplishments only to meet with disappointment in the realities of[60] life? Do you seek to win greater self-possession, more self-confidence,[70] greater powers of command? Do you sound unconvincing in argument?[80] Are you, in short, suffering from an inferiority complex? In[90] your dreams, your subconscious mind fondly overestimates your possibilities of[100] achievement and in your waking hours your fully conscious mind[110] under-estimates your possibilities, leaving you with a sense of your[120] own worthlessness, your own inability to accomplish anything of real[130] usefulness. This probably leads to sleeplessness at night or wakefulness[140] in the early morning hours. Many years ago I became[150] concerned with my own reactions to the many contacts of[160] life. I was developing a "sleeplessness" complex, and felt urgently[170] in need of some kind of mental stimulus. It happened[180] that shortly afterwards I met a psychological expert, and my[190] life was transported on to a new and exciting plane.[200] I learned to understand the gropings of my mind, to[210] understand the complex construction of that instrument of thought, and[220] very soon I was able to take constructive as well[230] as experimental action on my own account. I found the[240] study of psychological processes irresistible, and have since devoted my[250] life to it. I am convinced that most of our[260] troubles, physical and mental, are self-made, and that a more[270] complete command of our mental forces would confer great rewards[280] upon us. Consequently, I have now compiled a psychological work[290] which will help all those who feel that they are[300] groping along blindly in an atmosphere of hostility and hopelessness.[310] I am attaching to this letter a sheet giving full[320] particulars of this work, which costs only three guineas cash[330] or, if it is more convenient to the purchaser, may[340] be obtained by paying forty weekly instalments of two shillings[350] each. A study of this work will bring you an[360] enormous reward. Yours in friendship, Edward Hastings. (367)

(105) Edward Hastings, Esq., 17 Pavement Buildings, Brickyards. Sir, A number[10] of people have complained to us that you are forwarding[20] to them literature regarding a highly priced psychological work of[30] your own authorship and that you are constantly

suggesting that[40] the unconvincing matter contained in this book constitutes a magnificent[50] opportunity for self-improvement and advancement. We have taken constructive advice[60] and can confidently inform you that your manner of conducting[70] your concerns constitutes a nuisance to the majority of recipients.[80] The worthlessness and even harmfulness of your publications cannot be[90] made too widely known to the general public, and we[100] are now requesting you to complete and return to us[110] the accompanying document immediately. If you do not comply with[120] this request we are under definite instructions to take further[130] steps without delay. Yours faithfully, (135)

" C." Vocabulary for Outline Drill

commending	introductory	instrumentalist	cheating	championship
community	introspection	inhabitants	coughing	censorship
comply	magnanimous	inhale	castings	forgetfulness
complacent	magnetize	inhospitable	sweepings	credulousness
contributing	magnitude	illiterate	acceptability	boundlessness
contemporary	transmission	illiberal	advisability	stalwart
comparison	transfer	illegible	hospitality	awkward
reconnoitre	transgress	irresolute	novelty	dockyards
reconnoitring	translate	irrevocable	theological-ly	inconvenience-t-ly
recumbent	transplant	immeasurable	physiological-ly	transform-ed
reconcile	transcend	immortal	resentment	introduction
recognition	transaction	immortalize	refinement	magnetic-ism
inconstant	self-evident	emigrate	sentimental-ly	inscribe-d
inconsistent	self-defence	immigrate	fundamental-ly	inscription
accommodate	self-confident	hoarding	incompetently	
accompaniment	self-righteous	prying	persistently	

Dictation Practice

(106) (a) The lecturer persistently pursued his championship of a more liberal[10] education for all classes. It was, he claimed, self-evident that[20] a population which acted in an inconsistent, irresolute, and incompetent[30] manner could not, when the time came, be self-confident in[40] the matter of self-defence. He recognized completely the magnitude of[50] the task of giving complete instruction in the duties of[60] citizenship to every member of the community, but he considered[70] that such instruction would transform the entire life of the[80] country in a surprisingly short space of time. It was[90] with resentment that he listened to speeches which were a[100] fundamental criticism of the advisability of such instruction. Immeasurable and[110] irrevocable harm was done to the nation when the masses[120] were deliberately kept semi-illiterate. We must reconcile ourselves to the[130] fact that general recognition of this need for a more[140] liberal education is a necessary accompaniment to our progress as[150] a race. Many people in authority were too complacent, and[160] they exhibited a fundamentally unsound distrust of the abilities of[170] the commonplace person. The lecturer continued by stating that he[180] had entered an ordinary working class home recently. The inhabitants[190] of that humble home had been most

hospitable to him[200] in every way. In the corner of the room he[210] had noticed a bookcase containing an assortment of books which[220] he could only regard with astonishment. Among them were books[230] on Citizenship and on theological subjects; there was a large[240] book called *A Complete Introduction to Modern Science*, and a[250] book on the nature of Magnetism. There were sentimental books[260] and books of general interest. Among the titles which he[270] had jotted down were: *Country Contentments*, by Marcus Woodward; *Self-*[280]*Selected Essays*, by J. B. Priestley; *Adventures in Friendship* and[290] *The Friendly Road*, by David Grayson; *Contemporary Personalities*, by the[300] Earl of Birkenhead; *The Immortal Isles*, by Seton Gordon; *A*[310] *Quartette of Comedies*, by H. G. Wells; and *The Rover*,[320] by Joseph Conrad. A little questioning revealed that the man[330] had a son who some years ago had won a[340] scholarship, and during the years of his training he had[350] bought many books. These books interested his father so much[360] that he had read them all and had achieved a[370] very considerable measure of self-education.

The lecturer said that he[380] would continue to contend that the boy or girl from[390] the poorer home could derive considerable benefit from a more[400] liberal education. He advocated education on more rational lines, the[410] principal subjects taught bearing a direct relationship to life itself.   (420)

(*b*) constabulary concomitant phrenological accommodated self-congratulatory incomprehensible jocularity inhibitions dauntlessness associateship confiscated communal skilfulness indivisibility magnificently supplemental intractability introverted feasibility devastating

PART TWO: Omission of Consonants ; Intersections

"A." Vocabulary for Outline Drill

danger	attempt	call attention	new authority	national bill
endanger	political party	overseas bill	this month	railway
respect-ed	Labour Party	electricity	to-morrow	company
expect-ed	savings bank	company	morning	to meet
objection	new bank	form of agreement	trade mark	requirements

Dictation Practice

(107) The announcement of the increased rates was made in the[10] House of Commons yesterday when it was stated that British[20] Railways would increase all railway rates by ten per cent[30] as from the end of this month to meet the[40] requirements of the new situation. As was to be expected,[50] this announcement was not received with pleasure by any of[60] the political parties. The principal objection came from the leader[70] of the Labour Party who stated that, while the Labour[80] Party respected the need for meeting present-day requirements by[90] special action, they wished to call the attention of Government[100] officials to the fact that this

considerable increase in rates[110] had been agreed upon between the railway authorities and the[120] Government without any attempt being made to get the views[130] of the different political parties in the House. The crisis[140] had given Government officials very wide powers in many respects,[150] and it was necessary for Members to watch the actions[160] of these officials to make sure that they did not[170] use their new authority in the wrong way. Such methods[180] would endanger the state of good-will which at present existed[190] in the House. In answer to this objection it was[200] stated that it had been necessary to act quickly because[210] there had been a loss on railway working for some[220] time and the longer this loss continued the greater would[230] be the danger of having to increase railway rates to[240] a far bigger degree than was suggested now. It was[250] probable that they would be required also to increase the[260] rates for road services during this month.   (267)

" B." Vocabulary for Outline Drill

adjustment	production	Pitman's	local	liberal
postal	garden party	Journal	authorities	measures
mistake	various parties	Smith & Co.,	twelve months	railway
prompt	Professor	Ltd.	ago	passengers
substitute	Smith	County	on Saturday	growing
distinct	London Bank	Council	morning	requirements
anxious	City Bill	Colonel	high-water	Conservative
suspect-ed	draw your	Benson	mark	Party
passenger	attention	medical form	friendly society	please make
demonstrate	silk	recent	national	arrangements
demonstration	department	valuation	arrangements	

Dictation Practice

(108) Some shorthand writers, in their attempts to reach high speed,[10] make the great mistake of acting on the assumption that[20] they can cover up an inability to put correct outlines[30] down on paper promptly by substituting for that ability a[40] wild use of phrasing. They attempt to join many outlines[50] together with a recklessness which quite disregards the legibility of[60] the resulting forms. That this is a mistaken assumption is[70] amply demonstrated by their subsequent inability to read these long[80] and indistinct forms. Shorthand writers who are anxious to make[90] the fullest use of phrases in their speed writing should[100] pay close attention to the rules for phrases, applying these[110] rules wherever possible and adapting them when necessary to their[120] own special requirements. The general rules meet the requirements of[130] the majority of shorthand writers, and in their early attempts[140] to reach speed students should phrase according to rule and[150] not try to invent their own phrases. It is a[160] mistake to imagine that high speed writing is achieved because[170] the writer makes a greater use of phrasing. For the[180] most part, high speed writers suspect "fancy" phrases and promptly[190] reject any outlines which might be "dangerous" in subsequent transcription.[200] The principle of intersecting

in phrases is a particularly useful[210] principle because phrases formed as a result of intersections are[220] very distinct, and mistakes seldom arise from such forms. It[230] is very much worth the student's while to get a[240] thorough knowledge of intersecting forms and to apply that knowledge[250] when writing from dictation.   (254)

(109) Messrs. George Baker & Co., 4 Bank Chambers, Westbourne Terrace,[10] London, W.2.

Gentlemen, We have to thank you for[20] your prompt attention to our telegram of yesterday. Immediately we[30] received your account we suspected that there had been some[40] mistake, and we shall be glad if you will make[50] the necessary arrangements for the adjustment of this account at[60] the earliest possible moment. In our books here we keep[70] our own accounts quite distinct from those of our subsidiary[80] company, the Westbourne Production Co., Ltd., as we are anxious[90] that the shareholders of each company shall receive a proper[100] valuation of their interests. We shall be glad therefore if[110] you will make arrangements on similar lines in your Accounts[120] Department.

We should like to call your attention to some[130] very interesting experiments which we have made in our Research[140] Department recently. These experiments have resulted in our producing a[150] substitute fabric of excellent quality, and we propose to start[160] production almost immediately. We offer a strong invitation to both[170] Colonel Baxter and Professor Thompson to call here on Thursday[180] morning of this week at ten o'clock when we can[190] arrange to demonstrate to them the qualities of this new[200] substitute fabric. We are confident that this demonstration will interest[210] the various parties concerned, and should you receive a favourable[220] report from Colonel Baxter and Professor Thompson we should be[230] delighted to enter into friendly arrangements with you for the[240] marketing of the fabric. Please let us know by telephone[250] whether or not the suggested day and hour will meet[260] the requirements of these gentlemen. Yours sincerely, The Western Production[270] Co., Ltd.   (272)

" C." Vocabulary for Outline Drill

adjunct	pumped	Professor	Borough	Major General
instinct	messenger	Robinson	Council	assurance
distinction	retrospect	Thames	captain of the	society
conjunction	ministry	Embankment	ship	national
domestic	destruction	Finance Bill	investment	contributions
substitution	administrate	early attention	corporation	liberal payment
nevertheless	administration	to the matter	form of	we will arrange
notwithstanding	administrative	Yorkshire	examination	railway rates
ratepayers	monstrous	Department	annual	it is required
unprincipled	manuscript	Journal of	valuation	conservative
denomination-al	obstruction	Education	various	measures
incandescent	opposing party	limited liability	authorities	
contempt	Unionist Party	company	every month	

Dictation Practice

(110) (a) Ratepayers seem to harbour an instinctive contempt for the administration[10] of their Local Authorities in every department of life, and[20] most administrative offices arouse distrust in one form or another.[30] Nevertheless, one rarely hears any criticism of the Post Office[40] and the postal services generally. The regular distribution of letters,[50] parcels, telegrams, etc., is a wonderful tribute to the effectiveness[60] of the Post Office administration, and the Post Office plays[70] an enormous part in meeting the domestic requirements and the[80] public requirements of the community in the matter of communication.[90] In this connection there is a most interesting book called[100] *Messengers for Mankind*, published by Hutchinson, which deals with the[110] various forms of communication between men. The section which gives attention[120] to the development of the Post Office is particularly interesting.[130] In the early days there was a monstrous lack of[140] system in the sending and delivery of letters, and improvement[150] came slowly and along conservative lines. In 1581[160] the Government appointed a "Chief Postmaster of England" and an[170] improvement in the arrangements of some of the postal departments[180] of the country began. At that time the general postmasters[190] were usually inn-keepers whose horses were hired for the[200] use of Royal messengers. About twenty-five thousand letters were[210] dealt with by the London Post Office each week. To-day[220] the Post Office handles over twenty million letters a day.[230] The name of Rowland Hill is well-known to most[240] people for, notwithstanding unprincipled opposition and obstruction, he managed to[250] bring about the introduction of the penny post. Some authorities[260] were afraid this would involve a loss of revenue but[270] the Government took a more liberal view, and in[280] 1838 a committee of the House of Commons expressed[290] unmistakable approval of the measure. At the same time, the[300] use of "stamped covers" was recommended, and the use of[310] the stamps was made compulsory.

There was an immediate and[320] enormous increase in the number of letters dispatched through the[330] postal services, and to-day the Post Office is an immense[340] institution, demanding the attention of many thousands of employees. The[350] Travelling Post Office, known as the T.P.O., which[360] allows letters to be sorted during a journey and so[370] saves many hours in delivery time, was also introduced in[380] 1838. The first Travelling Post Office consisted of[390] a horse-box temporarily fitted up for use as a[400] sorting carriage, and began by running on the Grand Junction[410] Railway between Birmingham and Liverpool.

One feature of particular interest[420] is the private Underground Railway organized by the Post Office.[430] It is six and a half miles in length, carries[440] postal packets as passengers, and is self-operated. (448)

(*b*) Caledonian Railway Fascist Party Haberdashery Department Municipal Authorities Military Authorities Worcestershire Corporation Vauxhall Society Major Ramsbottom fastidious requirements liberal assumption worsted department Wallasey Corporation Journal of Anthropology Journal of Etymology Evolutionary Society Independent Party notwithstanding the fact